# TRAVELING WITH DOGS

## BY NONA KILGORE BAUER

Imagine being able to go anywhere in the world and bring along your best friend! This Quarterly steers you in that direction—vacations with your dog; traveling by automobile across state lines to hotels, parks, dog shows; into the woods camping, hunting and hiking; making reservations to go by airplane, bus, train, and more. This is a century on the move, and dogs have become a very important part of all of our lives. Are you ready to include your dog in your yearly travel plans? Find out all the details of traveling and get on the road to great times with your canine pal!

## WHAT ARE QUARTERLIES?

Books, the usual way information of this sort is transmitted, can be too slow. Sometimes by the time a book is written and published, the material contained therein is a year or two old...and no new material has been added during that time. Only a book in a magazine form can bring breaking stories and current information. A magazine is streamlined in production, so we have adopted certain magazine publishing techniques in the creation of this Dog Quarterly. Magazines also can be much cheaper than books because they are supported by advertising.

## QUARTERLY

yearBOOKS, INC.
Dr. Herbert R. Axelrod,
*Founder & Chairman*

Neal Pronek
*Managing Editor*

Barry Duke
*Chief Operations Officer*

Andrew De Prisco
*Editor*

yearBOOKS are all photo composed, color separated and designed on Scitex equipment in Neptune, N.J. with the following staff:

DIGITAL PRE-PRESS
Patricia Northrup
*Supervisor*

Robert Onyrscuk
Jose Reyes

COMPUTER ART
Patti Escabi
Sandra Taylor Gale
Candida Moreira
Joanne Muzyka
Francine Shulman

ADVERTISING SALES
Nancy S. Rivadeneira
*Advertising Sales Director*
Cheryl J. Blyth
*Advertising Account Manager*
Amy Manning
*Advertising Director*
Sandra E. Cutillo
*Advertising Coordinator*

©yearBOOKS, Inc.
1 TFH Plaza
Neptune, N.J. 07753
Completely manufactured in
Neptune, N.J.
USA

Cover design by Sherise Buhagiar

There are few places dogs enjoy more than inside your car. Whether you're taking your dog for a ride to the post office, into the woods to grandmother's house, or South of the Border, make sure your canine friend is comfortable and safe. Protect your seats with cushions that are dog-proof and washable.

# CONTENTS

The author thanks the many dog travelers who contributed their ideas, experiences and pictures to this book. It was great fun being "on the road" with other folks who enjoy traveling with their dogs as much as I do. Over the years my own vehicles have grown with my dog family. Eons ago I graduated from the traditional four-door family sedan to a regular pickup truck, then to an extended cab pickup, to the third-door extended cab truck we now own, purchased when my senior Golden Retriever retired to cab status.

Since my vehicles revolve around my dogs, it's apparent that I seldom go anywhere without them...*all six of them!* They have been my inspiration for this book.

Photography by Wendy Ballard, Nona Kilgore Bauer, Tara Darling, Ozzie Foreman, Isabelle Francais, Douglas Grevatt, Judy Iby, Mary Jong, Karen Taylor.

Special thanks for the courteous photograph contributions of Pet Affairs, Kennel-Aire, Hatchbag, Kennel Spring, *DogGone*™ newsletter, and Novalek, Inc.

Find out the safe ways to travel with your dog—his life is far too precious than to risk it by driving without proper restraints and safety measures. Sussex Spaniel, owned by Pat and Karen Cottingham and Diane Hudson.

# FOREWORD

It's as ancient as humankind itself—humans with their canine counterparts, whether Eskimos, Indians, Bedouin shepherds, or frontier pioneers, by sled, covered wagon, Oldsmobile, or Audi. Today you pile your family into the station wagon and head for the hill country or the shore. Maybe Disneyland, Cape Cod or the South of France. Family expeditions (now called vacations) are an old-time tradition, and those treks often include the family dog.

But is that a recipe for disaster? You wouldn't dare...your dog's a nut case in the car. Or maybe you've tried it and everyone was miserable. So you're leaving your pooch home next time.

Hold it! If you don't or won't travel with your dog and wish you could, this book is for you. It's also for those who do travel with their dogs but suffer nightmares along the way. The

On a trip to the Grand Canyon, Sparky the Beagle and the family breathe in this photographic view. Photograph courtesy of Wendy Ballard, publisher of the *DogGone™* newsletter.

**This Keeshond puppy is getting acquainted with his crate before embarking on his first long trip with the family. Owner, Kameo Kennels.**

information in this book can transform those trips into happier times for dog owners and, most importantly, the dog.

This book will not only address the obvious issues about dog transportation, it also will offer information on all aspects of pet travel and answer questions you never thought to ask. If you travel by car, how can you make a long trip fun and pleasant for your family *and* the dog? Should you fly with your dog and how safe is it? How should you identify your dog while traveling and how can you ensure his safety away from home? What do you pack for a dog? Will motels and hotels accept your dog and how can you make him welcome there? What kind of vacation

would you and your pet enjoy together? How do you handle an emergency on the road? What should you do if your dog is injured or becomes lost during your vacation? Can you and your dog travel abroad together?

These pages also include advice from seasoned dog owners who have traveled thousands of miles campaigning their dogs in competition. You'll gain a wealth of travel knowledge reading about their dog travels and dog paraphernalia.

Dog owners love to share their canine experiences and pass along all sorts of information from the important to the insignificant-but-handy. We invite you to travel with us to that end.

# SHOULD YOU TRAVEL WITH YOUR DOG?:
## QUESTIONS TO ASK YOURSELF

You reach for your car keys and your dog whirls into a tap dance around your feet. You open the door to the garage and your dog darts between your legs and bounces over to the car or truck, bounding to leap inside.

No doubt about it...most dogs love automobiles. A 1995 Gallup poll reported that fully 75 percent of dog owners treat their pets with rides in the car. To a dog, the car means going "out," a visit to McDonald's and a bit of burger, maybe an ice cream cone. Whether a short trip to the park or a two-hour jaunt to cousin Jane's, most dogs enjoy, indeed thrill, to accompany their humans in the car.

Now you're taking a vacation or planning an extended getaway weekend. Two weeks to Disneyland or the Grand Canyon, maybe a few days at the shore. You've studied road maps and pondered airline schedules. You've double-checked your packing list and bought new sunglasses and extra sunscreen. But there's still one nagging, unresolved issue...**Should you take your dog?** Your good buddy would love to tag along, but he might complicate your trip. You could leave him at home with a relative or friend, but you know you'll be miserable without him. Should you board him with your veterinarian or at a kennel? He could be just as unhappy without you. Should you take your dog along?

Your dilemma is not unique. Every year thousands of vacationing dog owners worry about what to do with their canine family members. Boarding kennels and pet sitters are possibilities, but pets can get bored and lonely without their people and familiar surroundings. And pet owners often spend most of their vacation missing their dog's companionship and worrying about the dog and his well being.

**Not every pooch will think a major excursion is a dandy idea. Is your dog ideally suited to traveling with the family? Dandie Dinmont Terrier, owned by Richard L. Yoho.**

Here's the good news! With judicious planning and proper canine preparation, your family dog can join the fun. The family can vacation together *and* enjoy quality time with their dog (...at least *most* of the time).

However, before you rush out to buy the dog his own travel bag, you should do two things. First, make an honest (*really* honest) appraisal of your dog. Not all pets are suitable traveling companions. If your dog passes muster, then take a realistic look at your travel plans. Sit down

with your family or traveling entourage and discuss the nature of your vacation, then weigh the advantages and inconveniences of sharing it with your dog.

Your canine "reality check" should first address his age. How old is your dog and would he handle the stress of extended time away from home? A young puppy who has not yet completely adjusted to his new home does not possess the social skills or emotional maturity to handle a variety of new surroundings over a short period of time. Pups under four or five months of age might be happier left with their breeder or at home with a reliable pet sitter.

Some older puppies who are charged with youthful exuberance easily become stressed if confined for extended periods. Think about the way he loves to zoom in circles around the yard or how he bounces into the mailman every day. Before you commit to an extended trip with your rowdy youngster, test his reaction to brief travel experiences with day-long family outings. Take him to parks and other public areas. Do these excursions send him into a frenzy of excitement? Would you spend most of your vacation calming him down? Even a more mature young dog who is emotionally equipped for a family vacation may need "practice" day-long jaunts before he could handle an entire week or two on the road.

Is your dog too old or frail to make a lengthy trip? Senior dogs who are inactive and prefer to snooze in sunspots all afternoon would not enjoy sleeping in strange motel rooms or climbing in and out of the car at rest stops on the interstate. An older dog who suffers from arthritis may have difficulty climbing in and out of a vehicle for frequent potty stops. Bumpy roads or long periods of confinement in a car or crate might cause discomfort to a dog with achy joints. Thus an older pet may be happier left behind with a friend in the comfort and security of more familiar surroundings.

Does your dog have any health problems that might cause difficulty on an extended trip away from home, a physical impairment or condition that would make traveling arduous or uncomfortable? Is he on any special medication? Talk to your veterinarian about your dog's medical needs and discuss the propriety of taking him on a trip.

Is your dog affected by motion-sickness? If he usually becomes ill or vomits during extended car trips, he'll surely bless you with more of the same on your vacation. Review your travel plans with your veterinarian: would he advise a long trip or prescribe medication to control the problem? Make several practice runs of varying lengths while using the medication to make sure it works. Otherwise, you will feel as miserable as your dog when he starts to heave on your new lambskin car seat covers. Dogs seldom become ill conveniently at rest areas; most often it happens while traveling at 65 miles an hour on a crowded highway without shoulder access. It's best to leave a chronically carsick dog at home. Always feed your dog at least two hours before leaving as a precaution.

Is your dog a seasoned traveler or does he become anxious or apprehensive when riding in a car? Some dogs view an auto as the enemy and tremble at the slightest hint of hopping in. If you use the three "Ps" of dog conditioning...praise, patience and persistence...you could turn his attitude around.

Begin with short daily rides, offering praise and reassurance the moment you turn the engine on. Use plenty of sweet talk during the ride; give him his favorite treats when he displays even a bit of calm behavior. Bring his favorite toy or blanket to bolster his morale. Make these test runs often, increasing the length of each trip. Most dogs quickly adapt to life on wheels. Then be honest in your appraisal of his travel behavior. If he doesn't respond positively, he'll be happier left at home.

Is your dog adaptable, confident and outgoing? Does he exult in visits to the beach or to parks filled with happy noise and lively children? He will encounter strange people, sights and sounds on your vacation. Will he welcome dog-friendly gestures from strangers or will he fret at every unfamiliar turn? A shy or poorly socialized dog will stress easily and wish he were at home beside your easy chair. An aggressive or overly protective dog who resents strangers and feels he must guard the family could be a threat to other travelers. Of course he doesn't mean it, but is your vacation worth the risk?

Is your dog obedience trained and well behaved? A traveling dog should be trained to sit, lie down, stay and be quiet on command. An unruly animal will frustrate the family, annoy other travelers, and make all of you unwelcome at your destination and checkpoints along the way. Ill-behaved and out-of-control dogs are the main reason many hotels and motels no longer accept guests with pets. Some facilities have had such unpleasant animal experiences that they won't even allow dogs in vehicles parked overnight in their parking lots.

If your dog is too rambunctious to travel, it's not too late for a short course in obedience to teach him mannerly behavior. Your veterinarian, local humane society or park district can recommend a good obedience class. Private trainers are another option, but will be more expensive. Group training is more advantageous as it provides an opportunity to socialize your dog in new situations and with other dogs.

**Some dogs are ready for anything! On the road for adventure, here's a quick-peddling Yorkie.**

**Will your active dog have lots to do in your chosen vacation spot? Sporting dogs and high-energy breeds (like Dalmatians) need plenty of daily exercise.**

Now evaluate your trip and destination. Will your pet's "vacation" include activities he will enjoy, or will it offer nothing more than lonely hours spent in a crate or a motel room while you explore the theme park, museum or planetarium? Also consider the fact that wherever you travel, there will always be places where dogs are not allowed... restaurants, pool areas, and other indoor attractions. You'll have to plan ahead for each eventuality. For your dog's sake, you have to know where he'll be or where you can house him during every moment of your trip.

Where are you going on your vacation? A city holiday filled with sightseeing, shopping trips and fine dining will not be fun or appropriate for your dog. He would spend too many hours crated in the hotel, most likely longing for the peace and privacy of home. Vacations to beach areas, country cabins, or other casual places with outdoor activities lend themselves naturally to dogs and provide a happier environment for families with pets.

Will your trip allow time to walk and exercise your dog? A proper dog-friendly vacation should include enough time to incorporate meal and airing schedules that most closely follow your dog's routine at home. If you satisfy his inner clock, he'll more easily tolerate other interruptions.

Does your destination have areas where you can walk your dog for exercise and elimination needs? A narrow strip of grass along a motel parking lot may serve your dog's purpose occasionally, but during a week or two on the road, he will need a safe place for walks and an area for exercise to release pent-up energy.

Is your hotel or motel nestled in a quiet country setting or is it surrounded by heavy industry or commercial businesses? Most city-raised dogs are accustomed to normal urban activity and noise, but the farm or country dog who is not conditioned to heavy traffic and noisy crowds could be unhappy, indeed frightened, in such an unfamiliar setting.

When do you plan to travel and what kind of weather will you encounter during your trip? Your dog will enjoy cool mountain air and breezy lakes and shores; he may not thrive in regions where the climate is hot and humid or extremely dry.

There is the added danger of heatstroke if your dog must be left in the car for any reason, even for a few minutes. On a warm day, a closed car, even one parked in the shade with the windows cracked several inches, can heat quickly to over 120 degrees and become an oven to the dog left inside unattended. In cold climates, the temperature inside a closed car drops quickly, creating an instant refrigerator. Your dog could succumb to hypothermia, lower-than-normal body temperature, in a very short time. Short-coated and toy breeds of dogs are especially vulnerable. Don't take those risks. Without extra effort and special precautions, weather extremes can turn your dog's vacation into a nightmare.

In some cases, pets who should not travel or are unable to do so comfortably may be better off in a boarding kennel or left at home with a relative or professional pet sitter. Most sitters will visit the home several times a day to feed and exercise the animal. If you decide to use a pet sitter be sure to check one or more references and interview the prospective sitter as thoroughly as you would a baby-sitter. Ask about prior experience and observe how the sitter interacts with your dog. They should be comfortable with each other before you go away. You should leave detailed written instructions on your pet's routine and stress the importance of following his normal schedule as closely as possible.

For more information on locating a professional pet sitter, there is an American organization that you can call known as the National Association of Professional Pet Sitters at 800-296-7387. Another helpful organization called Pets Are Inn finds "host families" who will board your pet while you're away. Their number is 800-248-7387. Boarding kennels are another option as well.

Sparky the Beagle gets around...and doesn't even have to paddle. Here's Wendy Ballard's family canoeing in Oregon. Photograph courtesy of the *DogGone™* newsletter.

# BEFORE YOU LEAVE:
# A VISIT TO YOUR VETERINARIAN

Several weeks before your departure, take your dog to your veterinarian to make sure he's in good health and can handle the rigors of a road trip. Update his immunizations and obtain a health certificate and proof of rabies vaccination. You should keep current copies of his health records in your vehicle glove box at all times, not just during your vacation, in case of an emergency or unexpected trip. State laws vary on rabies control, so you need to take a complete immunization record with you. You may never need to show them, but if they are required and you don't have them, you could be asked to contact your veterinarian to FAX copies to the local authorities, which could be inconvenient, time consuming and expensive. Emergencies are always unpredictable. If your dog needs to see a veterinarian during your trip, his medical records could be a lifesaver.

**A visit to your veterinarian is in order before taking your dog on a long trip. Do your homework and find out everything about the area that you're planning to visit. Your vet can alert you to any health concerns particular to your vacation spot. Owner, Chris Parker.**

Tell your veterinarian where you're planning to travel and ask about any communicable diseases that may be prevalent in your destination area. Inquire about Lyme disease, Erlichia, and Rocky Mountain Spotted Fever if you will be hiking or walking in heavily wooded or grassy areas where you and your dog could encounter any of the several varieties of ticks known to transmit disease to dogs and humans. Your vet can also suggest and dispense a sedative or prescription in case your dog becomes a restless traveler. (The American Society for the Prevention of Cruelty to Animals suggests avoiding tranquilization. If

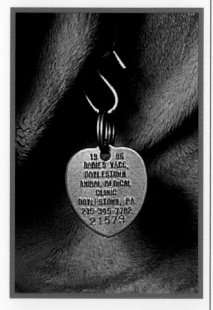

**Attach your dog's rabies tag securely to his collar, along with his ID tag with all pertinent information.**

the dog becomes overly stressed by traveling, they recommend your leaving the dog at home.) *Never give your dog human medication prescribed for nausea or motion sickness.* It's dangerous and could be fatal for the dog.

Be sure the rabies tag and an identification tag are securely attached to your pet's collar in case you become separated while you're away from home. The "S" hooks that come with most ID tags are easily bent and lost, so as an extra precaution, you might substitute a small keyring to attach the tags. You should also attach an extra ID tag with the name and telephone number of a relative or friend. After all, if your dog gets lost during your vacation, you won't be home to take the phone call when someone finds him (but be sure that you've left your answering machine or service on, just in case).

# IDENTIFICATION AWAY FROM HOME

When you travel, you should also carry good-quality photographs of your dog, head shots as well as full front and side views. In case the worst happens and he becomes lost, you can photocopy the pictures and post them in veterinary offices, animal shelters, gas stations and other heavily traveled public places. A written or verbal description is never as effective as a photograph.

Attach a complete written description of your dog to the photographs before you leave home. Don't rely on your memory if your dog becomes lost or stolen. In a state of panic or confusion, you may forget the white streak down his chest or the ragged notch on his left ear. A good description of your dog should include the following: call name, breed or breed mixture, sex, age, tattoo or ID number, collar type and color, coat description (including hair length and texture, color and markings), weight, height at shoulders, description of ears (erect, cropped, drooping) and tail (long, short, bushy, cropped, curly), and any other special markings or scars. Often owners include relevant medical information, such as "Needs Daily Medication." Whether true or not, this kind of plea may heighten the public's compassion and dampen the potential dog-napper's notion of a big-money reward for your beloved "expensive" purebred dog.

**Microchip is a popular method of identifying dogs permanently. The microchip is a computer chip about the size of a grain of rice.**

## PERMANENT IDENTIFICATION: TATTOO YOUR DOG

The best means of pet identification, the one popularly recommended by veterinarians and dog professionals, is the tattoo, a permanent number placed on the inside of the dog's rear leg. You can use your Social Security number or the dog's AKC registration number, then register that number with one of several tattoo registries. A tattoo immediately identifies a dog as someone's pet and alerts the veterinarian or animal shelter who may come in contact with the dog. Stories abound about lost dogs returned to their owners because of a tattoo. Tattoos are also a major deterrent against dog theft, since tattooed dogs will not be accepted for use by research labs and are less likely to euthanized at an animal shelter. Bring attention to the tattoo by adding it to your dog's ID tag, stating "Dog tattooed."

The National Dog Registry is the nation's largest and most widely used tattoo registry and has registered dogs and other pets since 1966. You can obtain complete information about NDR and tattoo registration by writing Box 116, Woodstock NY 12498, or calling 914/679-2355.

As of 1995, dogs with tattoos also may be enrolled in the AKC Companion Animal Recovery Program. This program is not the same as AKC registration; you must enroll separately.

**This dog is tattooed on the inner thigh, as well as identified with a microchip. The owner chose his Social Security number to identify his Golden Retriever, then submitted that number to the National Dog Registry. The number is also registered with the AKC "Home Again" Companion Animal Recovery program.**

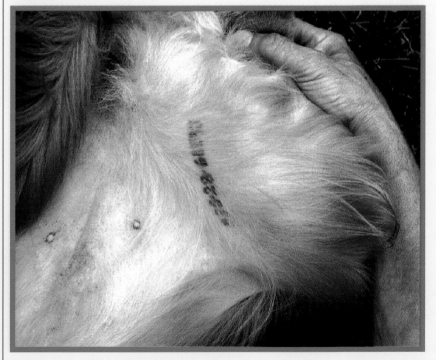

## MICROCHIP IDENTIFICATION

Like tattoos, microchips are another permanent way of identifying your dog. The canine microchip is a tiny computer chip about the size of a grain of rice, encoded with a series of permanent characters of information that identify the dog forever. The chips are completely passive, having no batteries, power supply or moving parts, and are encapsulated in the same type of glass used in prosthetic devices for humans.

The microchip is injected into the soft tissue between the shoulder blades in a completely safe and painless manner. The chip will not migrate from that site, and because it's housed in a biologically inert material, it will not harm the host canine. The implant must be done by a veterinarian or a trained professional. Microchip identification is done through a hand-held scanner.

While the technology is relatively new, microchipping has rapidly gained acceptance and approval as the best means of pet identification. In 1995 the AKC announced it had joined forces with Schering-Plough Pharmaceutical Company to provide a nationwide animal-identification and recovery program. Schering-Plough will market the Destron microchip, under the name "Home Again" through veterinarians. Any animal identified with the Destron microchip is automatically enrolled in the AKC recovery program. AKC provides the database management service for Schering-Plough and several other microchip manufacturers to provide a national pet identification and recovery service under the name AKC Companion Animal Recovery. As database manager, AKC provides 24-hour-a-day toll-free-number service for recovery. The best protection for your dog might be a chip *and* a tattoo. Your veterinarian can advise you on both.

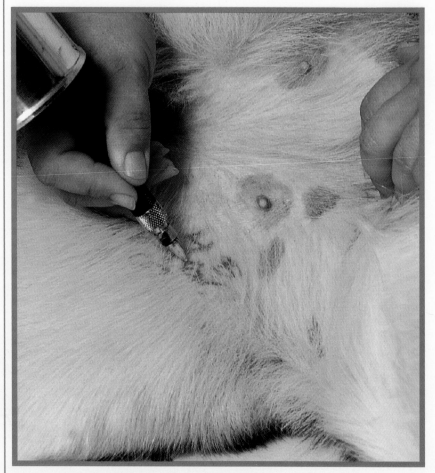

This dog is being tattooed for permanent identification, a major deterrent against theft which has grown increasingly common for all dogs, not just show dogs.

The microchip is painlessly implanted between the dog's shoulder blades. When scanned, the microchip will trace the dog to his owner.

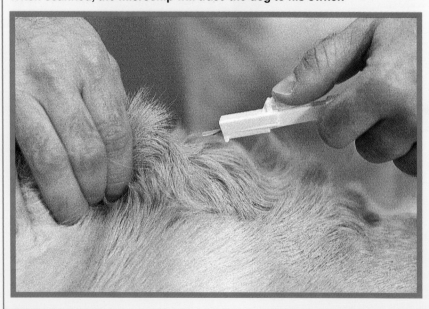

# TRAVELING BY CRATE

**Although your dogs would rather bound around your station wagon, chew on the gear shift, and sit on your lap while lapping bugs through your windshield, here's the safe way for your dogs to enjoy a Sunday ride.**

## CRATE ADVANTAGES

A dog crate is your best investment for your dog's automobile travel safety. The dog crate is like a baby's car seat; it will help protect the dog in case of accident while at the same time provide a traveling den where the dog can relax (therefore so can you) or take a nap. While en route, your dog will be confined and won't be able to jump in your lap, nuzzle your neck or roughhouse with the kids. A loose dog in a moving car is unpredictable and causes accidents.

Every state has a law requiring the driver and passengers to wear a seatbelt while in a moving automobile. The law is equally strict for children under four years of age or under 40 pounds; they must travel in a car seat. Your canine traveling companion runs the same risk and should be afforded the same travel safety as other members of the family. Unsecured, he could sustain some type of injury during an accident or sudden stop. Restless or very active dogs are even more at risk and can injure themselves just bouncing around in a moving automobile.

In the U.S., as of 1995, only California and Oregon had laws requiring safety restraints for dogs in vehicles, and several other states had introduced legislation mandating pet restraints. Pet crates and pet seatbelts satisfy that requirement. Both devices ensure safe travel whether on vacation to the Grand Canyon or on a short trip to the vet. As a safety-conscious driver and caring dog owner, you have a responsibility to crate or buckle up your dog before you roll down your driveway.

If you don't already own a dog crate, purchase or borrow one to use as a traveling den for your dog. It should be big enough for him to lie down and turn around comfortably. Crates fit easily in the back of most minivans and station wagons. In some larger passenger vehicles, a crate will fit on the back seat of the car.

A few years ago a truck carrying four dogs was involved in a serious single-vehicle accident. The four dogs crated in the truck bed under the topper survived without a scratch. A bit shaken and wild-eyed perhaps, but not a paw out of place, thanks to their wire crates wedged tightly together in the back of the truck.

The crate will also serve double duty while you're on the road by providing a safe haven for your dog once you reach your destination. By crating your dog when you leave your cabin or motel room, you prevent him from soiling the carpet or causing

**Domino, a Siberian Husky owned by Erica Beradi, poses beside a crate that's just the right size for him.**

damage to motel property. Most importantly, your dog will feel secure in his own den while he's in strange surroundings. Most property damage occurs because the dog feels stressed at being left alone and becomes destructive due to separation anxiety.

Crating also eliminates the risk of your dog's running out of the room if a maid opens the door to clean your room and accidentally permits the dog to escape. It also spares the maid, who might be terrified of all excitable four-pawed guests. If the dog must be left alone and/or uncrated for any reason, place a "Do Not Disturb" sign on the door and inform the front desk of your situation.

Many motels and hotels welcome dogs if they are confined to crates. Crating demonstrates responsible dog ownership and ensures that the pet will not be a menace on the property or become a nuisance to other hotel guests. When making reservations at any facility, always advise them that your dog is part of your entourage and will be safely crated at all times. Ask if there are any special pet restrictions. Some facilities won't offer maid service if there's an animal present, even one that's crated. Just reassure the management that your dog will not be a problem...and then make sure that he isn't!

Crates are available in pet-supply stores, pet shops and discount stores. Some wire-mesh crates collapse suitcase style to fit easily into the trunk of most cars. Airline-type plastic crates are often less expensive, easier to handle, but are somewhat less ventilated. Your vehicle type and available space will help determine what type of crate you can use for your dog.

**This talented, crate-trained Husky is showing us how easy it is to get in and out of the right crate.**

### CRATE TRAINING FOR TRAVEL

Your dog should be "crate-conditioned" before you attempt a long journey together. If your dog has never been crate-trained or hasn't spent time in his crate recently, don't just plunk him into a crate on the day you leave and expect him to understand and settle in like a professional traveler. Your vacation could become a daily battle with a very stressed and unhappy dog. In order to be successful, crate training must be a positive experience for the dog. He must not view the crate as a punishment or other negative. You can start crate introduction by tossing a cookie into the crate for him to retrieve and eat; do this frequently before closing the crate door behind him. Once he's comfortable entering the crate, you might feed him a meal or two in the crate, first with the door open, then with it briefly closed, to further establish this crate business as a pleasant experience.

Use a kennel command such as "Kennel" or "Crate" when he enters. Don't lavish heaps of love and attention before you crate him, rather just give him a pat or two and a small treat to make this a low-key procedure. Use "Good boy, crate" to tell him he's a good fellow when he gets in. His release from the crate should also be uneventful and normal, with just a casual welcome and a scratch behind the ear. Never call the dog to you, then immediately put him in the crate, or he'll soon make that association and resist coming when called.

Under no circumstances should you use the crate as punishment for naughty behavior—no matter how strong the temptation to "send him to his room." Your dog will forever view his crate as a bad place with unpleasant memories.

Over a two- to three-week period, extend his crate time until he's spending at least an hour in the crate. Make sure he's quiet in your absence by waiting out of sight where the dog is unaware of your presence. He must learn to be quiet while crated alone or he'll disturb other guests wherever you stop or stay.

Complete information on the whys and hows of crate training a dog can be found in a good many books on puppy rearing, especially *A New Owner's Guide to Training the Perfect Puppy* by Andrew De Prisco, published by TFH. Another excellent resource is the pamphlet *A Pet Owner's Guide to the Dog Crate* published by the Nicki Meyer Educational Fund Effort, 31 Davis Hill Road, Weston, CT 06993.

**Sadie is a three-month-old mixed breed who happily demonstrates how the crate works! See!**

### CRATE TYPES AND CRATE ALTERNATIVES

If you travel in a minivan or full-size van, you will probably find crating the most convenient way to travel for both you and the dog. The crate becomes a "den within a den" and most dogs learn to enjoy traveling in a crate because they associate it with being with their favorite people and doing something fun. For your own peace of mind, a crate safely and comfortably protects your dog from injuries caused by sudden stops or accidents. Even at speeds as low as 30 mph, an unrestrained dog can be killed if thrown against the dashboard or through the windshield.

The ideal travel crate for dogs under 30 pounds is made of lightweight, high-impact tinted plastic that protects the animal from sunlight but is clear enough so you and your dog can see each other. It's well ventilated and has no sharp corners to damage the interior of your car. Best of all, you can secure it with the seatbelt in your car. Crates for larger dogs come in wire mesh or sturdy plastic material.

All plastic pet carriers approved for airline transport are suitable for automobile use. They have large ventilation slots or holes and are easy to assemble and clean. For versatility, the door can be removed so that the crate can be used as an open shelter, or the top can be removed and the bottom section used as a pet bed. Typical sizes are: 12 inches wide by 20 inches deep and 15 inches high, suitable for small breeds of dogs; 17 inches wide by 24 inches deep by 20 inches high, for medium size dogs such as Poodles, Beagles, Pekingese or Dachshunds; 21 inches wide by 30 inches deep by 24 inches high, for slightly larger dogs like Shelties, Bulldogs and Cocker Spaniels; 23 inches wide by 35 inches deep by 26 inches high, for medium-large dogs such as Doberman Pinschers, Labrador and Golden Retrievers, Dalmatians, Collies, Boxers and German Shepherds; 26 inches high by 42 inches deep by 30 inches high, for large dogs like Weimaraners, Afghan Hounds, Alaskan Malamutes and Old English Sheepdogs.

Very large breeds such as Mastiffs, Great Danes, Newfoundlands, St. Bernards or Irish Wolfhounds will probably require specially constructed crates. These would be necessary for airline travel but would be impractical or impossible for most vehicles.

Crates in similar sizes also are available in several gauges of wire mesh. Most of these break down to suitcase size, and several brands offer a fold-and-carry cage that collapses in minutes into a flat, portable package with a carrying handle. Metal crates offer the best ventilation and see-through traveling comfort for a dog. Most are equipped with bottom trays or pans. Toss in a comfy blanket or large towel for your dog to snuggle into for the ride. Wire mesh crates and plastic carriers are available at most pet supply outlets and through pet-supply catalogs.

**A crate is the safest means by which to travel with your dog. Accustom the young dog to the crate, and he will easily accept the crate for trips anywhere.**

### EMERGENCY INSTRUCTIONS

In case of a serious accident where you are rendered unconscious or unable to communicate with emergency personnel, your dog crate should have a set of instructions attached to it for the rescue people at the scene. By the time a rescue person looks through your wallet and finds information about your dog, the dog could be on his way to a pound or shelter with no one to follow up on his behalf. If you're badly hurt, it might be days before you can take action. In most accidents involving animals, rescue workers take them to the local shelter or humane society. Many facilities only keep them for three to seven days before the animal is euthanized.

You can protect your dog from this kind of tragedy. Attach a plastic sleeve to his crate (to each individual crate if there is more than one dog) and insert a 5 by 8" index card with emergency instructions for anyone who finds your dog. The card should have your name, address, telephone number and an alternative contact in case you're unavailable. You might also include special information on how to calm the dog and any verbal commands the dog responds to. You should add instructions to "Please leave dog in crate to remove from auto." A frightened dog released from a crate by a stranger could bolt unexpectedly into traffic or out of sight. Caption the card EMERGENCY NOTICE and state, "All costs associated with the veterinary care and boarding of this dog will be reimbursed in full. A reward (indicate amount) will be paid to the person who accepts the responsibility of this dog until the owner or designated alternative caretaker is contacted and the dog returned to them." Sign the card and if possible, have it certified by a notary public.

The Orlando Dog Training Club distributes a comprehensive emergency notice for travel crates. We thank them for allowing us to include it in this book.

One final crate reminder. Don't travel with food or water bowls or other

**So that your dog can enjoy the countryside and still be protected... from accidents and ultraviolet rays, here's a tinted, high-impact plastic carrier, suitable for dogs under 30 lbs. The crate includes a cushion and can be fastened to the seat with a seatbelt through the bottom.**

large hard objects in the crate. They can turn into flying missiles during an accident or sudden stop.

**These are four popular sizes of traveling/training crates, suitable for airline travel as well as car travel. These plastic crates can be purchased in any pet-supply house.**

# DOG-SAFE STUFF FOR YOUR TRAVELS

### PET SAFETY SEATBELTS

If you don't want to crate your dog while driving and prefer to use a restraining device, you have several choices. The car safety harness or seatbelt system gives your dog the same type of protection as a seatbelt gives the driver. The pet seatbelt is made of nylon webbing and comes in small, medium, large and extra-large sizes and is available through pet-supply catalogs. Several types have foam-padded chest straps. Simply strap the harness around the dog, then slide the seatbelt through the harness loop. Certain belts have an adjustable safety strap with one end fashioned to buckle into the existing seatbelt with the other end clipping onto the pet's harness. This will allow some movement while the pet is safely restrained.

Once the harness is on the dog, it also becomes an accessory-attachment for a leash extension, allowing the dog to remain securely fastened in the harness even while out of the vehicle for

Wearing a standard harness with a nylon leash, this is Sandridge's St. Elmo's Fire. The harness slips into any car seatbelt.

exercise during pet stops along the way. This restraining device is suitable only for auto use and cannot be attached in the bed of a pickup truck.

If you opt to use a seatbelt harness, don't wait until the moment of departure to put it on the dog. Test it beforehand for proper fit on the dog as well as in

the car, and to be sure you've purchased all the components. These are not complicated to fasten and attach, but if you're missing a strap or buckle, you'll need time to replace that part. A pre-trip test will also acquaint the dog with the restraint so he won't become apprehensive when he's strapped in.

### DOGGIE CAR SEATS

If you own a small dog weighing 10 pounds or less, you might consider a pet car seat, a canine barcalounger of sorts. Also available through pet-supply outlets, the pet car seat is a canvas-like box that attaches to your car's seat with the automobile seatbelt and can be adjusted to different heights to allow your dog to see out the window. The seat also includes its own seatbelt for the dog. Small dogs seem to relish riding in their little throne-like seats where they can sit near their person and watch the rest of the world zip along the highway.

The seatbelt harness attaches easily to the seatbelt of your car or truck.

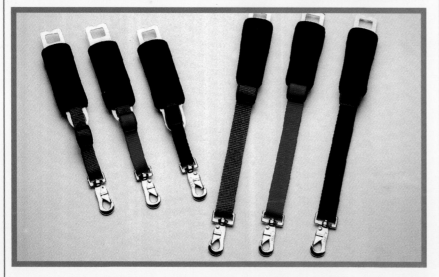

**This Siberian Husky looks dapper and safe in his harness, ready for a long trip with his owners.**

### BARRIERS AND DIVIDERS

If you drive a station wagon or hatchback vehicle, a third option is a barrier that confines your dog to the rear of the vehicle or van. Metal barriers are usually made of expandable aluminum or steel mesh panels and installed by adjusting the tension on two threaded rods. They do not restrain the animal: your dog could still be thrown about during sharp turns or quick stops, so drive safely. Similar barriers are available for sub-compact cars and standard sedans.

A netting device made of one-inch square nylon mesh is similar to the metal barrier and is sized specifically for most vehicle and model types. It mounts behind the front seat, or rear seat in some vehicles, and attaches to the molding of vehicles with a dual-lock hardware system that requires no drilling. It will also combine with the cargo area liner to protect your vehicle as well as your pet. The liner is constructed of heavy-duty, vinyl-clad waterproof polyester fabric that resists tearing. It attaches easily to the interior of your vehicle with Velcro™ strips. As with the metal barrier, it will not restrain your dog in case of an accident.

You can protect the floor of your minivan or hatchback vehicle, in fact even the seats, from muddy paws and doggie accidents with disposable protective liners. The four-foot by seven-foot protective mat is durable, absorbent and leakproof.

For total safety, many dog travelers crate their dogs in the partitioned area. The dog can stretch his legs safely in his own barricaded space during lunch and rest stops, then return to his crate during actual road time. The combination is up to you!

### WINDOW GRILLS

The dog equipment manufacturers have covered all the security bases with window grill devices. If you're worried about fresh air and ventilation for your dog without the dangers of his head out your car window, you might add a window ventilation grill to your auto travel accessories. These plastic grills come in two sizes, adjustable for window widths up to 24 inches or up to 40 inches, and are easily installed or removed. The grill is inexpensive protection for the dog who loves to hang out the window, sniffing the breeze…as most dogs do. As refreshing and exciting as sniffing the breeze may be for your canine passenger, his eyes, nose or ears can be injured from bits of flying debris and the incessant rush of air. Your dog could even push through an open window at the

**This spaniel sits contentedly behind a safety barrier designed to keep your dog in the rear part of your vehicle. The width of the three-piece barrier can be adjusted to fit any size vehicle and is an ideal dog-divider for most minivans and station wagons.**

tantalizing sight of a squirrel, cat or another dog. Window grills eliminate these dangers.

They also offer continuous protection when your vehicle is stopped for any reason and your dog might be tempted to dangle out the window while he waits.

### TRUCK RESTRAINTS

Love your dog? Do not allow him to ride unsecured in the back of your pickup truck. It's not only extremely hazardous for the dog, but in many states it's against the law. By 1995 four states, California, Massachusetts, Oregon and Washington, and several counties in Virginia and Florida had passed laws mandating the restraint of pets in open-bed trucks, with similar legislation pending in several more states.

**Never travel with a loose dog in the back of a pickup truck. This is very dangerous for your dog—and you value his life much more than the price of a restraint! A pickup truck restraint will keep your dog securely attached in the bed of your truck.**

Regardless of the law, it is irresponsible and dangerous to transport an animal unrestrained in an open truck bed. One statistic shows over 100,000 dogs are killed and thousands more injured every year due to riding in open pickup trucks. Most are thrown from moving vehicles during a sharp turn or sudden stop or start. Even a quiet dog sitting or lying down unsecured is at risk of being thrown about

**These Golden Retrievers have been "netted" in the back of this minivan. This netting device attaches with simple Velcro-type closures and keeps the dog confined to the back of the vehicle.**

and injured. Unsecured dogs also pose a threat to other motorists who may be involved in an accident when the dog jumps, falls or is jarred from the truck bed onto the roadway.

Don't let your dog become a statistic. There are safe and comfortable restraints available for "truck dogs." One cable system uses a short cable to connect the dog to an aluminum track that is mounted on the truck bed. The cable has a plastic slider that allows light movement while preventing the dog from jumping or falling out. These should be installed with caution because with too much range of motion, the dog can hang himself over the side of the truck.

Look for the pickup truck restraint that requires no special installation and consists of a triple nylon strap. Two end straps clip onto the tie-down rings or existing eye bolts on the side of

the truck bed, and a short center strap attaches to the dog's harness and restrains the pet.

The truck bed should be covered with a slip-resistant covering that will provide safe footing for the dog as well as insulate the bed from extremes of heat and cold. The driver riding cozily inside a heated or air-conditioned truck cab may not notice his dog in back doing a tap dance on a frigid or over-heated truck bed.

**Be sure to protect the floor of your vehicle from any doggy accidents. A liner designed especially for this purpose can be purchased from pet-supply houses.**

# CREATIVE TRAVELING

**A washable seat cover, available from most pet-supply houses, is your best bet to keep your furry friend's fur off your car seats.**

The word "minivan" is almost synonymous with canine travel. Without a doubt, it has become the vehicle of choice for the family who travels with children or dogs or both. Dog exhibitors and competitors as well as companion dog owners hail the minivan as the most comfortable and versatile method of motoring with dogs.

There are as many ways to equip a minivan for travel as there are people who drive them. Jackie Lutz of New London, Missouri travels extensively showing her Border Collies in obedience competition. She's picked up most of her best travel habits through her own unfortunate experiences and

**A double crate, extra room for your dog or for two dogs together, fits nicely in the rear of a small pick-up truck. Photograph courtesy of Mick and Yvonne Pertle.**

warns dog travelers to look beyond convenience and anticipate the consequences.

"I packed so much so often that I finally put a chest of drawers in my minivan," Jackie said. "The first time I packed the dresser and drove away, the drawers flew out at the first turn we took, and I barely escaped death from the chest itself when it followed the drawers in my direction." MINIVAN LESSON NUMBER ONE: Secure all large and loose items to the vehicle floor or walls.

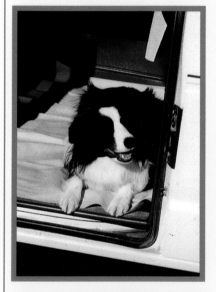

**Dandy the Border Collie, relaxing comfortably in the back of owner Jackie Lutz's minivan. Protective pads can be purchased to keep muddy paws off the floor.**

Jackie's creative attempt to keep her van carpet clean also backfired. She laid a sheet of plastic over the carpet and taped it to the sides of the van wall just above the carpet. The tape welded itself nicely, but her Border Collies tore up the plastic and during the ensuing frolic, clouds of Border Collie hair flew about. Jackie was stuck with unremovable furry tape permanently affixed to the van walls.

Indiscriminate and careless packing has also resulted in Panalog™ ointment dripping into Jackie's cosmetic bag and

**Two crates fit easily in the rear of this minivan. A battery-operated fan mounted on the top of the crate keeps Chaser and Sally cool on a long trip. Owner, Martha Blank.**

rawhide chew bones crunched in her boots. Jackie's best advice: "Anticipate and plan ahead!"

If you own a standard-size sedan and long for the convenience of a station wagon or minivan, you might appreciate how Kevin Kilgore of Schaumburg, Illinois, refurbished his four-door sedan. Kevin removed the rear seat from his car, then covered the rear floor with a platform made from two-by-four lumber. He attached a sheet of three-quarter-inch plywood over the top, covering the entire floor area where the back seat had been. That elevated wood floor was then covered with heavy-duty, snag-proof carpet. Kevin's dogs could jump into the car with ease and had their own "room" to stretch out in during rest stops. While traveling, they were also restrained with harnesses attached to the car's rear seatbelts. The open rear area was

also spacious enough to accommodate one or two large crates if necessary.

Mick and Yvonne Pertle of St. Louis often travel with their two Golden Retrievers and one small mixed-breed dog. To maximize the space in the rear of their Jeep Cherokee, they removed the back panels on two retriever-size wire-mesh crates and wired the two open ends together, making one very long crate. The three dogs most agreeably share the crate space and enjoy traveling together. On cold days, you'll often find them snuggled together in a heap to share their body heat as well. The Pertles leave nothing to chance where their dogs are concerned. They bolted the crates to the inside of the Jeep bed to prevent sliding around during sharp turns or sudden stops. They also padlock the crate doors and lock the tailgate when they have to leave their dogs unattended in the car.

# THE DOGGIE TRAVEL BAG: WHAT TO PACK

**What to pack! Let your dog decide, and he'll take all his favorite toys from Nylabone®. Keep in mind that your dog will need lots of entertainment on vacation, and his selected chew toys—Nylafloss® and Gumabones®—will occupy lots of good chew time.**

When you pack your own bags, put together a special travel pack for your dog. Include his favorite blanket or sleeping mat, food and water bowls, and his own supply of drinking water. A sudden change in water can cause diarrhea in some animals, and that would dampen everyone's vacation spirit. If you find yourself running out of water on the road, experienced dog travelers suggest using a gallon jug of tap water from home and replacing small amounts as the water is used. The new water is gradually diluted with the original water, which prevents a sudden transition to the new water. You can also use bottled water for convenient and complete protection. Some experienced dog fanciers say that adding a few drops of fresh lemon juice to a dog's drinking water while traveling will prevent stomach upset and diarrhea. You can also purchase non-spillable water dishes so your dog can have splash-proof access to water in the car.

Bring enough dog food and special treats for the entire trip rather than attempt to buy it en route and discover that they're unavailable. A sudden change in diet, especially in a strange place, could really upset your dog. If you are forced to change your dog's diet while traveling, do so in small increments. Add small amounts of the new food at each meal while decreasing the proportions of old food. A gradual change will lessen the risk of digestive upset from the new food.

Include a few large bath towels, a roll of paper towels and clean-up supplies in case your dog gets sick on the trip. Be sure to pack his favorite toys and chew objects so he can indulge himself during long hours of travel or crating. Nylabones® and Gumabones® are excellent stress-satisfiers for a traveling dog, and Nylabone® Frisbees™ provide fun chase-exercise between periods of confinement. Also pack a comb and brush and dog shampoo. While dog baths usually are not included in most vacation plans, it's wise to be prepared in case your dog digs or rolls in something smelly. Nasty dog odors can hang like a heavy cloud in automobiles and motel rooms...you could lose a good night's sleep and leave a lasting impression on the motel management.

Also pack a bottle of flea and tick spray in case you run into unwelcome visitors on the road. If your trip includes hiking or backpacking, you'll need to check your dog after each outing for foxtails, seeds and ticks. Brief grooming sessions during your trip will keep him free of critters and make him easier to live with in close quarters. And you know

**A spill-proof pet watering container holds up to two gallons of water. It can be laid on its back and the water still remains inside without spilling a drop. Simply turn the unit upright and the trough fills and maintains a water level of about two inches.**

how much he'll enjoy the extra time and attention.

Don't forget to bring your canine good citizen equipment, a scooper and a generous supply of plastic baggies for picking up your dog' stools at motels and other public places. The reason he is welcome at your destination is because previous dog-owning guests cleaned up after their dogs. Many establishments no longer accept dogs because inconsiderate people failed to poop-scoop after their dogs. Don't become part of the problem.

Most importantly, be sure to pack every dog's best friend, his leash. The leash will keep him safe and under control when you take him out of the car at gas stations or parking lots and roadside areas where traffic is a hazard. A leash is essential for all doggie potty stops and will prevent your dog from becoming a pest to anyone whom he might meet during his airing and exercise periods.

The leash will also protect your dog on walks in parks, campgrounds and wooded areas.

**Exploring the countryside with her owner, this setter is safely under control on a retractable lead. These flexible leashes are ideal for walking your dog, for exercise and romping about when on vacation.**

New creatures abound in strange surroundings, and if you happen upon a strange dog, a snake or porcupine, you'll be able to keep your dog under control and out of danger. Unless you are on fenced private property and have specific permission for your dog to run loose, he should be leashed at all times while out of the car or at a motel or campground.

As an alternative to the standard 6-foot leather leash, you might try a retractable long line available in lengths from 8 to 20 feet. These flexible devices offer a larger exercise and roaming perimeter while still maintaining that all- important aspect of complete control. They're great for the owner who doesn't need as much exercise as his dog does!

Include a first aid manual in your canine travel kit for fingertip instructions on how to treat for heat prostration and other unexpected accidents. While few problems occur on a well-planned trip, experienced dog owners learn to expect the unexpected.

**Retractable leads come in a variety of length and strengths, suitable for dogs of all sizes.**

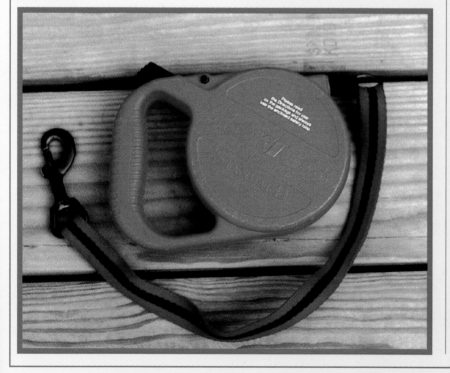

**The Doggie Bag**
- Favorite blanket or sleeping mat
- Food and water bowl
- Gallon jug of tap water from home or bottled water
- Leash and retractable lead
- Dog food and treats
- Bath towels, two or three
- Roll of paper towels
- Favorite toys, Nylabones®, Nylabone® Frisbee™
- Brush and comb
- Dog shampoo
- Flea and tick spray
- Plastic baggies and/or scooper
- First-aid manual
- First-aid kit

# ON THE ROAD: PLANNING YOUR VACATION ROUTE

Plan your vacation route carefully to allow no more than four hours between rest stops so your dog can relieve himself regularly. Offer him water at each stop. Keep a supply of fresh cool water available at all times. Plan his main meal for the end of the day when the family is settled down for the night.

Never allow your dog to run loose at rest areas; always keep him leashed. Some newer rest stops along interstate highways have erected outdoor runs or pens where travelers can leave their dogs during food and potty breaks.

If the weather is extremely warm, you might choose to travel before 10 a.m. or after 3 or 4 p.m., the cooler parts of the day. Dogs don't cool off by perspiring the way people do and have difficulty coping with hot climates.

Above all, never leave your dog alone in a parked car on warm days. Heat prostration develops quickly and can lead to brain damage and death. If your dog becomes uncomfortable from the heat, prepare damp cool towels for him to lie on. If he develops heat prostration, wrap him in cold wet towels and get him to a veterinarian as soon as possible. Consult your first-aid manual.

It's so easy to become distracted on vacation and forget your dog is waiting in the car. That wait can be a fatal one—don't risk it! Factor in the very real possibility of dog theft and you'll never leave your dog alone again!

**On the road with Sparky and Wendy Ballard.... any great vacation takes planning. Be prepared and informed and you and your dog will have a doggone great time! Photograph courtesy of DogGone™ newsletter.**

**DOGGONE GOOD INFORMATION**

Published by Wendy Ballard of Vero Beach, Florida, *DogGone*™ is a newsletter for people who like their dogs, like doing things with their dogs, and like their dogs enough to want to vacation with them! Wendy says, "Kick the kennel habit!" Take your beloved dog on vacation with you. The quarterly newsletter (which is subtitled "The Newsletter About Fun Places To Go and Cool Stuff To Do With Your Dog") gives first-paw advice about places to go with your dog, and not to go, with recommendations about lodging, campsites, safety precautions, and more. These folk are so doggone into travel and have so many great ideas about places to go and things to do that interested travelers should take advantage of this handsome little publication. In just a dozen pages four times a year, *DogGone*™ takes you and your dog around the country, citing neat sites and sights for your whole family to enjoy. Subscribe by writing to Wendy Ballard, *DogGone*, PO Box 651155, Vero Beach, FL 32965-1155 or at BallardDG@aol.com.

### MOTELS, HOTELS AND PET VISITORS

A complete listing of motels and hotels that allow pets is listed in the Gaines publication *Touring with Towser.* It can be ordered from Gaines booklets, TWT Gaines Professional Services, P.O. Box 877, Young America MN 55399. Some automobile clubs also publish lists of pet-friendly facilities. The Humane Society of the United States offers reprints of a four-page article on "How to Travel With Your Dog." You can order it from HSUS, 2100 L St. NW, Washington D.C. 20037.

Some motels charge an additional fee if you bring a pet into your room. Others require a refundable deposit. Most importantly, the individual innkeeper, not the franchise chain, sets the policy about pets. Additionally, many cities and towns have their own ordinances that prohibit the keeping of dogs and pets in the sleeping quarters of hotels and motels. It's always best to check with each facility to find out if pets are permitted.

**If you're accustomed to your dog sleeping on your bed, be sure to lay his own blanket on the bed to prevent him from soiling the motel's linens. Photograph courtesy of *DogGone™* newsletter.**

**Locate a motel that accepts dogs and be the most courteous guest you can be. Sparky is admiring the fancy tile work in this Florida motel bathroom. Photograph courtesy of *DogGone™* newsletter.**

### WHEN YOU ARRIVE; WHILE YOU'RE THERE

When you check in at the front desk, remind the desk clerk that your dog is with you and will be crated or on a leash at all times. Some proprietors like to meet all their guests, including the four-legged ones. Ask if there are any rules that apply to canine guests and inquire about special exercise areas for dogs. Are there any specific areas that are off-limits to dogs?

Also find out the name and whereabouts of the local veterinarian in case of an emergency, injury or illness. While most dogs travel without incident, surprises such as bee stings, snake bites, intestinal upset, deep cuts or other accidents often require immediate attention. You'll save valuable vacation time if you have emergency information in advance.

Be sure to ask if any pesticides, mouse or rodent poisons are used in the rooms or on hotel grounds. Bait traps are sometimes placed under the beds or other inconspicuous areas. Also inquire about weed killers and other pesticides used on lawns or grassy areas so you can avoid those treated areas with your dog.

Never allow your dog to drink the water from the toilet bowl (like it or not, it happens in the best of dog families...) in your motel room. Many facilities use chemicals to sanitize the stools. Keep the lid closed at all times and put your dog's own water dish in a place convenient for the dog where water splats won't do damage. Provide a mat or towel (your own) under the dish to protect the floor or carpet.

Out of respect for the next hotel guest, try to prevent your dog from sleeping on the bed or bedding. However if that's impossible because your dog is a bed dog at home, bring your own bed covering to keep dog hair off the bedspread, or bring a dog mat to put on the floor so he can sleep comfortably near you.

If you must feed your dog while in your room, bring along a mat to put his food bowls on. Dog food splattered on the carpet will leave a bad taste with the housekeeping staff and management for the next round of canine guests. Never use the ice bucket or ashtray for a water or feeding dish!

**To use plastic-baggy pooper-scoopers, place your hand inside the baggy, grasping a paper towel if desired. Pick up the stool and draw the baggy down over it and withdraw your hand. Tie the baggy and dispose in an appropriate container.**

**Whenever leaving your dogs in the motel room, be sure to crate them (separately, of course). Don't forget to put the "Do Not Disturb" sign on the door for everyone's safety.**

Try to avoid grooming or brushing your dog in the room, but if you must, be sure to clean up every puff of fur. Dog debris is difficult to clean up and is highly visible as well as unpalatable to non-dog guests and cleaning personnel.

Whenever you leave your hotel or motel room, be sure your dog is crated and hang the "Do Not Disturb" sign on the outside door knob. That will prevent hotel employees from entering the room and upsetting your dog or even releasing him from his crate. If the unspeakable happens and your dog damages motel property, always do the honorable thing and inform the management and offer to pay for replacement or repairs.

During your motel stay, take your dog for frequent walks to keep him limber and exercised (both mentally and physically). Vacations are to enjoy each other's company as well as view the scenery and local entertainment.

And don't forget the leash! It's canine safety and good manners and always a hotel requirement to keep your dog on leash at all times when on hotel property. Loose dogs can tromp the tulips, pester other guests and upset non-dog visitors. There's always the added danger the dog may bolt or run away in strange surroundings.

Never take your leashed dog into the pool area, lounge or dining room. You can safely assume all these areas are off limits to dogs and pets. Always walk your dog away from flower beds, ornamental landscaping and other public areas where he might damage shrubbery or annoy another guest.

When exercising your dog, respect the next guest who may walk that way and use the "scooper" and plastic bags you brought along. (For no-mess scooping, put your hand inside the bag, pick up the deposit, then pull the bag inside out away from your hand and over the waste material. If you prefer more protection for your hand, you can hold a paper towel before grasping the stool. Knot the bag and drop it in the nearest outdoor trash bin.

An obedience-trained dog will be welcome almost any place you choose to visit. You and your dog will set a good example and weave a welcome mat for future guests with well behaved dogs. An unruly dog who won't sit, lie down or come when called is just as obnoxious as the owner who screams and yells at his dog. Conversely, a mannerly dog who sits and stays is a joy to travel with and a pleasure to meet for the friends he'll make along the way. Those obedience commands could also protect him from injury or save his life in an emergency situation where an instant response might protect him from a dog fight or a speeding car.

**A Personal Message from a Motel Owner**

The best advice for people who visit hotels and motels with their dogs comes from a former motel owner. For 20 years Rosemary Frantz operated the Pines Motel in Driggs, Idaho. While most of Rosemary's dog-owning guests were pleasant and considerate, a few unfortunate experiences left indelible impressions. On one memorable occasion, two large retrievers slept in bed *under the sheets* with their owners, leaving an unsightly layer of black hair all over the bedding.

Even the most conscientious of dog families can use reminders now and then. Rosemary's letter to dog owning guests is reprinted here with her kind permission.

"Register your dog with the desk clerk, it is nice to know all the guests.

"A well groomed dog is attractive to all, not just the prospective motel owner. Keep your dog clean, dry and brushed. It takes time to remove all traces of a dog from a room.

"Does your dog sleep on the bed at home? If he does, please provide a complete bed covering for him. If he doesn't, please bring along his own clean rug or blanket so he will know where to sleep.

"Do you feed your dog on the carpet in your own living room? Feed him outside the motel room, or bring along a mat to put his own dishes on. Ashtrays are too small and they make the food taste awful.

"Please ask where to walk the dog. The children of the other guests have special places to play. The two are not a good combination.

"Since your dog is in a strange place, *never* leave him alone in the room. He will bark at every sound he hears outside the door. He will also try to get out of the room. This makes unsightly nail marks on the door, right below the knob. He isn't dumb, he knows how to open the door, but just can't do it.

"Keep your dog on a leash or under control at all times. That small child or elderly person may be bowled over by your friendly and lovable pet now capitalizing on his freedom from the car."

Rosemary Frantz

**Don't take advantage of your dog-friendly motel's good will. Find out where dogs are permitted and abide by the rules. Never try to sneak a dip with your inconspicuous Dane. Owner, Rob Wilson.**

# TRAVELING WITH SHOW DOGS

**Show dogs are often kept on show grounds in a transportable, collapsible wire pen, ideal for giving the dogs fresh air, visibility and security. This family of Shetland Sheepdogs is resting before their time in the ring.**

Traveling with conformation dogs may be considered the Cadillac of canine travel. Perhaps no segment of the dog fancy devotes itself more to canine luxury and convenience than the show-dog set.

While some show exhibitors stay at local hotels and motels during a show weekend, a huge number prefer to take up temporary residence on the grounds. Almost 100 percent of dog shows and obedience trials permits camping on the show grounds. Wander through the back lots and parking areas of most show sites and you'll find an instant mini-city populated with pup tents, customized RVs and $100,000-plus motor homes.

These dog show campers share more than a common interest in dogs. They have discovered that camping on the grounds offers increased safety and advantages and greater canine comaraderie.

They love the convenience of 24-hours-a-day on the show grounds where they can literally walk out their door and into ringside. While waiting for split ring times, they can "go home" and take a nap, prepare lunch and feed or walk the dogs.

Some show sites charge each vehicle a daily fee, others do not, and many who claim to charge a fee never get around to collecting it from their campers. Some provide a limited number of electrical hook-ups; water hook-ups are usually scarce. However, power and water are seldom a problem, since most of the RV population is self-sufficient and equipped with generators, water tanks and the latest in canine gadgetry. These capsulized homes on wheels allow more space for the

**The show dog's home away from home. RV travel is the choice of many conformation exhibitors because it offers all the comforts of home while still allowing them to be close to the dogs on the highway and at the show. Photograph courtesy of Bob and Betty Woerman.**

dogs...and their people...and provide greater security since the owners can spend more time with their animals. Forget the common card table and TV cart or stand. Most of the units are crammed with multiple dog crates, exercise pens, grooming tables, large floorsize fans and other paraphernalia designed to pamper the on-the-move show pooch.

Exhibitors also enjoy a freedom and individuality unavailable at a motel or hotel off the grounds. They bring portable grills and cookers and spend evenings under the awning, dining and visiting with their fellow exhibitors and friends, both human and canine variety. They can set up an exercise pen next to their trailer and create an instant portable backyard for their dogs.

**Inside the Tioga RV, six crates stacked for the canine passengers.**

Show dogs are designed to travel. Serious dog exhibitors are on the road 50 weekends a year, and that includes everything from cars to planes. Dogs that show frequently get used the rigors of traveling. Shih Tzu, owned by Debbie Burke.

Exercise pens are standard equipment on the show circuit. Given the variety of dogs, you'll find X-pens suitable for every breed and size of adult and puppy dog. Pens come in up to five different heights with connecting panels, and two or more pens can be hooked together to create more space. If you own large or active dogs, you can also attach top panels to prevent them from jumping out of the pen. Shade cloth covers, customized or "off-the-rack," will block out the sun and keep the dogs cool on sunny days.

There's rain protection as well. Many exhibitors use ground covers with their exercise pens. Made of tightly woven tubular polypropylene, the mats provide a smooth comfortable surface while still allowing rain and other fluids to pass through. The mats are easily cleaned by hosing or sweeping and roll up for convenient travel and storage.

Spring and summer dog shows boast a sea of colorful shade tents with prices ranging from very moderate to quite expensive for elaborate vendor-type tents. Smaller tents are advertised as "dining tents," lightweight yet big enough to cover one chair and a dog crate. One ingenious...and expensive...tent creation fits over the tailgate and pulls out into a screened porch that extends from the back of a van or station wagon. Some dog suppliers even offer collapsible gazebos made of nylon and netting that can be enclosed in bad weather.

Bob and Betty Woerman of Quincy, Illinois show Long-haired Dachshunds, Brittanys and Whippets in bench competition. On their ideal weekend, they pile their dogs and grandkids into their 21-foot Tioga RV and travel to dog shows in their three-state area. Bob and Betty and youngsters sleep in compact and fold-up beds; the dogs have their own customized arrangements. Bob constructed a permanent platform behind the driver and passenger seats that will accommodate up to nine small dog crates or six small ones and one Whippet-sized. The RV is permanently equipped with kitchen and personal supplies, and dog supplies of course, everything they need for road trips except the dogs.

Show campers suggest renting a camping RV or motor home to see if you like RV life before making a major investment, only to discover you prefer the Holiday

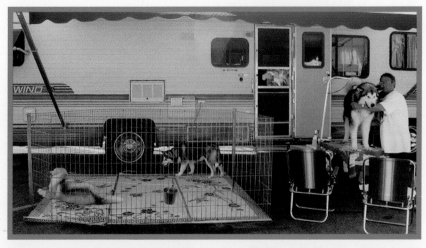

**Dean and Deb Fischer and their Alaskan Malamutes Sheba, Sultan and Awesome tour the dog-show circuit in a comfortable RV.**

Inn. Many started at the bottom, with a two-man tent or fold-down camper and graduated to 20- and 30-foot travel trailers. If you're curious, browse the camp sites at your show grounds. It's easy to make friends with dog folks, and if you're lucky, they'll give you a tour of their rig.

**Bullmastiff Spanky, owned by Jim and Deb McFarland, awaits his turn in the show ring.**

**Bob and Betty Woerman relaxing with two of their Dachshunds outside the Tioga at a dog show. Dogs shows are great opportunities to meet fellow dog lovers, and weekend shows provide lots of social time for the dogs and exhibitors.**

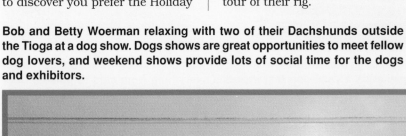

These Smooth Fox Terriers travel to dog shows in owner Jane Swanson's cargo van. They even have their own license plate "FOXTER-1."

Lightweight crates are easy to transport and provide shade for the dog inside. They are easy to assemble and collapse into a large envelope for carrying purposes.

Two Bearded Collies keeping cool and out of the way in their crates. Be sure your dog has plenty of circulation and water when being kept around the show grounds. Heat exhaustion is *very* common in dogs and must always be guarded against. Owner, Mary Ann Pflum.

This Golden Retriever puppy seems anxious for his first match!

Six Pembroke Welsh Corgis in crates fit easily in the back of a full-size cargo van.

Wire pens give these three outgoing show Beagles plenty of room to socialize and interrogate the photographer. Beagles, owned by Penny Kretchmer.

Samoyeds, owned by Charlotte Waack, enjoy classic travel accommodations to and from dog shows.

Here's the way *not* to travel with your dog in a pickup truck! The author's China demonstrates this traveling *faux pas*.

This content Australian Shepherd is properly attached with a pickup truck restraint. Tia, owned by Joann Menke.

A double crate created by connected two crates with the end panels removed and attached back to back can comfortably accommodate two dogs...if they're friendly!

Securing two crates in the back of a pickup truck is another way of safe travel in this type of vehicle. Owner, Joann Menke.

# TRAVELING WITH HUNTING OR FIELD TRIAL DOGS

**Modeling her camouflage swimwear, this is KC's Anything She Wants Lola. This vest keeps this little devil warm when swimming or retrieving in cold water as well as afloat if she tires.**

My Dodge Ram truck is a second home to my family of Golden Retrievers. Just drop the tailgate and all five dogs will leap up and jockey for position in their crates, ready to head off for the next training session, field trial or hunting test.

My husband and I travel a five-state circuit with our Goldens, running field trials and hunt tests. Truck inspection is a favorite pastime between series at field events, and we've picked up some great ideas to incorporate into our own truck arrangement. Over the years we've revised and upgraded our truck setup to accommodate our dogs' comfort as well as ensure their safety on the road.

The basic and most important part of our truck design is the raised platform in the truck bed. We built a full deck over the wheel wells, which expands the floor area for the dog crates, and most importantly, raises the crates to window level, allowing better air circulation around the crates during warm weather.

The deck is built from one and one-half sheets of four-by-eight-foot, three-quarter-inch plywood nailed to a framework made of two-by-four lumber, creating an almost six-foot wide by eight-foot long wooden deck. We covered the deck with a remnant of sturdy Berber carpet to prevent the crates from sliding around. As a bonus, the carpet is also a natural magnet for all the field debris the dogs track into the truck (not to mention all that Golden hair!). It maintains a neat appearance even when covered with grit and vacuums easily between trips. Twice a year I treat the carpet with a spray for flea control.

The truck bed under the deck is carpeted with indoor–outdoor carpet, although a truck bed liner would be the ideal protection for the bed. We also installed a heavy tailgate mat on the inside of the tailgate to provide better footing for the dogs, especially when they have wet or snowy paws. The rubber also presents a cooler surface during hot weather, when an open metal tailgate exposed to summer sun can burn a dog's foot pads as it jumps onto the truck.

The plywood tray beneath the deck is made from the leftover half-sheet of plywood used on the deck. It extends all the way to the front of the truck, giving eight feet of removable storage space.

**This pickup truck is outfitted to transport five field-trial retrievers.**

There's plenty of room for a full-size suitcase, a couple of folding lawn chairs to use in training and at trials, and several large dishpans of training bumpers. We also carry a double-bed size bedspread in a large plastic bag. Some motels allow dogs, and when one or two of our Goldens gets to "sleep in," we cover the bed to keep that Golden fur from bothering the next guest. We also pack several large towels for drying dogs, and fleece mats to line the crate bottoms for insulation during severe cold weather.

While we utilized the entire underneath area for storage, Connecticut field trialers Iveaux "Andy" and Julie Anderson designed their bottom storage area with slots and drawers planned specifically to hold a 20-pound container of dog food, holding blinds, small shotguns and training gear.

The fiberglass topper on the Anderson truck has a vented roof to provide extra circulation on very hot days. Andy designed a tool to open the vent without climbing inside under the cap. He attached a small copper washer to the end of a wooden dowel rod long enough to reach the roof. The washer fits snugly over the thumb screw which opens the roof vent. Just raise the rod, press and turn!

We topped our own truck with a raised or "wedge" cap to allow extra headroom for dog crates on the elevated deck. We chose an aluminum cap because, in the salesperson's opinion, the dents and nicks from our Midwest hailstorms (and overhanging branches, etc., out in the field) would be less apparent in the molded aluminum than on a fiberglass top, and the silver not only matches the gray truck body but also reflects the sun's heat and keeps the interior cooler in the summer. The aluminum, however, isn't sturdy enough to support installation of a vent on the roof of the cap.

Three crates fit snugly across the truck bed in front of the sliding window of the truck cab.

Rear view of the raised deck. The plywood tray pulls out to store suitcase and training equipment.

The storage tray pulls out for easy access to training gear.

Our first truck cap had standard sliding windows on each side, and during hot weather we worried constantly about adequate ventilation for the dogs. Our present cap has "shop" or carpenter's doors on both sides that open out to provide easier access to the crate area and allow full cross ventilation when we're parked. While driving in extremely hot weather, we prop the doors open with a training bumper tied to the door hinge, then secure the door in place by attaching one end of a bungee cord to the door handle and the other end to the side of a crate. That extra opening pushes a lot of air through the back of the truck. Some dog folks have designed a special hinge that will prop a side door partially open using a conglomeration of training gear.

The side and rear windows have gas powered brackets that keep them stable when open and prevent them from springing up too quickly. The gas brackets also help keep the side doors snug with the bumper props.

To allow even more air circulation while stopped or on the highway, we included a sliding window in the front of the cap. On 90-degree days, the additional air flow from the front slider and propped-open side doors helps cool the dogs and adds extra insurance against heatstroke.

To protect the dogs from exposure to the intense heat of direct sun, in spring and summer we cover the side and rear cap windows with a specially designed vinyl material available from a camping-supply catalog. Sold by the foot in 36-inch widths and easily cut with a sharp scissors to fit any size window, it's applied to the inside of the window with a squeegee or a wet towel. The laminate blocks out 70 percent of the sun's heat, glare and light; I've tested it myself, and it's at least 15 degrees cooler under the cap with the laminate on the windows. We simply peel it off when cooler weather arrives and pack it away for next year. Plastic auto shade is also available at national discount chain stores.

For extra circulation during extreme hot weather, we installed a battery-operated, 12-volt fan on each side of the front of the cap. The fans are mounted above the crates with off-on switches under the fan on the driver's side. They oscillate during operation so all five dogs enjoy the benefit from the additional air movement.

This custom vehicle has six boxes to house retrievers, plus a handy drop front platform for grooming and first-aid at the rear. FC-AFC Riparian Roughrider, owned by Cliff and Jeanne Garland.

Our raised deck worked best when we traveled with only four Goldens and used only two crates in each row. When we kept a pup from a litter a few years ago, we faced the challenge of fitting five crates into a four-crate setup. We replaced the two rear metal crates with two airline type crates and one smaller crate. Fortunately our youngest Golden is a small bitch and fits nicely in the smaller crate. To prevent the two front crates from sliding backwards, we slide a one-by-two across the deck behind the crates to lock them in position.

Each crate is equipped with its own two-quart stainless-steel water bucket, so the dogs never lack for water when confined. We had tried inexpensive galvanized metal buckets from the local hardware store, but they rusted and never cleaned up well. The stainless steel were expensive, but they wash up easily, keep the water cleaner and last long

**Real on-the-road ingenuity! Rear view of customized field trialers' truck, including compartments underneath a raised deck to hold dog food, guns and training equipment. The front section of the platform is divided into two storage areas serviced by trap doors accessible through the side windows. Photograph courtesy of Andy and Julie Anderson.**

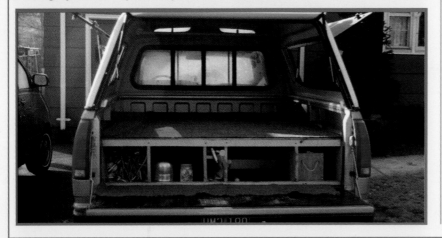

**Two crates fit sideways or lengthwise in the back of the truck. Water-resistant crate covers protect the dogs from cold and wind. The rear flaps also opens to provide better ventilation.**

Dog food is always a challenge to pack, depending on the length of the trip and the amount needed. For short hauls, we use five- and ten-gallon buckets, and on longer trips, we just pack the whole 40-pound bag. Plastic gasoline cans in the one- or two-gallon size (unused, of course) make ideal water carriers, although the most commonly used water carriers are still one-gallon milk jugs or large plastic detergent bottles (unscented detergent only!). During very hot weather, we freeze water-filled, one-quart soda bottles, and as they melt, the dogs have a continuous supply of cold water during a training session. We have also used those frozen bottles in the crates, like giant popsicles the dogs can lie on to cool off.

We carry our miscellaneous equipment and training supplies in a large covered plastic container that fits under the deck. Training pistols, shells and whistles, training collars and a

enough to make the investment worth it.

The crates trays are lined with thick, perforated rubber matting, the same type used in automotive shops. We buy it in three-foot-square sheets from a national discount chain and cut it to fit the crate bottoms. The mats are definitely our best "find." They allow wet dogs' to sort of drip-dry in their crates, and they help scrape the mud and gunk off the dogs' feet and undercoat. The dogs also never have to lie directly on a wet, hot or cold or dirty crate pan, and the mats provide a comfortable cushion for those long days spent at trials and hunt tests. Every time we clean the truck crates and hose a layer of mud and dog hair from under the mats, we're grateful all over again for those mats. No surprise that we've put them in all of our house crates as well.

Each crate also has its own padlock...possibly our most important crate accessory. At motels and restaurants, even at some hunt test sites, our dogs are always locked in their crates, inside the locked truck cap. With

animal rights extremists at large and dog theft on the rise, we feel strongly about taking every precaution to protect our dogs.

**Golden Retriever Leo, owned by Carla Schoepp, relaxes on his tailgate.**

leash for each dog, (important in case of a highway emergency), orange tape for marking blinds, paper towels, plastic bags and cups, and a complete first-aid kit equipped for field use. We always keep copies of the dogs' immunization records in the glove box, along with sunscreen and mosquito repellent. We've installed extra hooks in the truck cab to hold raingear and training jackets for cool and/or cold weather. A big umbrella fits nicely behind the truck seat, and two set of boots, short and tall, are permanent truck fixtures so we never drive off without them.

Most dog trainers and handlers love to show off their latest dog traveling innovations, and the ideas we've collected have improved our dogs' lives on the road and have always added to our own travel pleasure and convenience.

**This vehicle is equipped with a closet at each end for clothing, a breezeway for training gear, a bottom drawer for bumpers and a row of drawers for dog food and hunting paraphernalia on the passenger side. Photograph courtesy of Cliff and Jeanne Garland.**

**Close-up of the drawers on the Garland truck to hold various hunting and traveling needs.**

**Jasper TDX rests in the family Explorer after earning his final Tracking title.**

Crate lined with a heavy-duty rubber mat and equipped with a stainless-steel water bucket. A new 1- or 2-gallon gas container makes an excellent water carrier. The nozzle will reach through the crate mesh to fill water buckets without having to open crate doors.

Chip, a rescue Golden Retriever owned by Linda Huma, is an outdoor buff who enjoys snowmobiling. Chip is also a nationally known therapy dog who demonstrates for Paws with a Cause.

Sienna and Jasper show off their ribbons on their crates after successful performance in hunting and working tests.

# CAMPING WITH DOGS

If you're a dog-owning camping enthusiast, you might ask the question...who enjoys camping more, you or your dog? Of all the popular leisure and outdoor vacation activities, camping is the one best shared with your dog. From Dachshund to Great Dane, from Beagle to Bullmastiff, almost all dogs love the Great Outdoors. Is there a dog afoot who doesn't stalk a cricket or a butterfly? And even the daintiest of dogs relishes fresh grass beneath his paws. A camping vacation offers your good buddy a respite from the daily city grind and round-the-clock outdoor fun.

Whether you camp alone in the wilderness or at a campground with other camping buffs, you must be certain that your dog is trained and prepared to demonstrate his best behavior.

A dog who barks constantly, runs wildly through other campsites and digs or destroys native wildlife will not be welcomed by campers or campground operators and will probably be asked to leave. Much of today's strong anti-dog sentiment among campers and hikers is due to the fact that many people simply turn their dogs loose as soon as they reach the hiking trail. Loose dogs will frighten children and even adult hikers, spook horses and other pack animals, and intimidate other dogs who are leashed or who may try to rip your dog's face off. Today "No Dogs Allowed" signs are sprouting up at many state parks and other public grounds, largely because of preventable dog-owner behavior and dog problems.

An unruly dog also poses a significant risk to himself in an outdoor environment that allows more freedom of movement. Can you say with absolute certainty what your dog would do if he suddenly encountered a deer or rattlesnake, perhaps a bear? Veterinarians in popular camping and hiking areas report treating several dogs for snake bites every year, all of them running loose when bitten. Some survive, some don't.

Of course dogs have more fun when they're running loose, and in a perfect world we could allow them the luxury to chase and romp about. Unfortunately we are responsible for their safety and that means a collar and leash and good canine behavior when they camp or hike with us. If your dog is obedient and mannerly, he'll be a welcome addition to your own camping experience and a delightful new acquaintance for everyone who meets him. And he'll still have a splendid time!

## CAMPING PROTOCOL

Most national parks allow dogs as long as they are on a leash or tethered. Most state parks and many private campgrounds also welcome leashed dogs. Special kennel accommodations may be available in areas where pets are not allowed. You should check in advance to find out which parks and campgrounds allow dogs.

The American Automobile Association publishes for its members a "Camping and Trailering" directory that includes pet restrictions in its approved listings. Most campground directories will tell you which private facilities permit dogs. You may need to acquire a wilderness permit to cover the areas in which you wish to hike. You should call or write to the agency

**Rescue Goldens Kramer and Cassie, owned by Skip and Margaret Grevatt, are ready for the family's camping holiday.**

that administers the property, the Bureau of Land Management or the Forest Service office. A campfire permit will also be required if you plan to camp outside managed public campgrounds. Whenever you hike with your dog on well-traveled paths or on back country trails, you should observe the same rules of canine courtesy that govern dog visitors everywhere.

1. Most importantly, pick up after your dog! Use the plastic baggie "scoopers" to keep the trail clean for other hikers.

2. Keep your dog on a leash or long line and never allow him to run free or disturb other animals or hikers. The leash will keep him on the trail and prevent him from running into heavy brush or undercover where he could become injured. It will also safeguard native wildlife and plant life against damage from intrusion by a curious or rambunctious dog.

4. Keep your dog quiet and under control, especially at night.

5. On the trails, preserve your dog's good neighbor status by

**Camping in the San Juan National Forest in Colorado, here's Sienna and Jasper, owned by Ann McGuire of Texas.**

giving the right-of-way to other hikers who may be afraid of dogs.

6. Use your dog's backpack to clean up and carry any debris you might find along the trail. Always leave the trail and camp sites clean and ready for the next hiker or camper.

7. Watch out for your dog at all times. His welfare depends on you.

Observe a few health safety rules for your dog as well. Make frequent rest and water stops, called "refresh" stops in backpacker-ese. About once every hour, stop to rest in the shade for several minutes and give your dog a splash of water from your water canteen or the hiking bottle in his pack. Stop more frequently if the weather is hot or your dog appears tired and thirsty. Jane Morehouse of Hayward, California remembers a friend who took his older dog Maggie for a simple one-and-one-half hour hike in a local park with gentle sloping trails. He did not want to carry a bulky water bottle for such a short springtime walk. But it was the first warm day, and Maggie overheated and suffered a fatal heatstroke. Never underestimate the importance of a water supply for your dog.

Before starting on your trail hikes, treat your dog's legs, chest and underbelly with flea and tick spray obtained from your veterinarian. You can also spray your dog's top coat with a mixture of Avon Skin So Soft™ bath oil diluted about ten to one with water. Outdoor dog enthusiasts insist the bath oil works better than any dog product on the market. No one

**Shasta, owned by Ann McGuire, is exhausted after a busy day of camping.**

**Kaye Fuller, DVM demonstrates how to zip Lola into her swimming vest.**

knows *why* it works, only that it *does*. Rub the diluted oil into the dog's coat and put a stronger solution on the inside and outside of the dog's ears. Use it also to remove cockleburs from a heavy-coated dog. Spray it on full strength and let it soak a bit, and the burs will slide right out.

After walking or hiking in grassy fields or wooded areas, check your dog from nose to tail, especially between the toes, for cockleburs, seeds and foxtails. If he has run through tall weeds or heavy grass, also check beneath his upper and lower eyelids for tiny seeds that may have lodged under the lids. Scour his coat for ticks and other tiny mites that might have eluded your tick preventatives and hitched a ride upon your dog.

Be especially alert for symptoms of heat exhaustion and heatstroke if you're hiking during warm or hot weather. Both conditions occur when the dog's body is unable to cool down and his circulatory system overloads. If your dog succumbs to the heat or goes down, you will need to lower his body temperature as quickly as possible by immersing him in cool water or dousing his body with cool, not cold, water from a hose or other water carrier. Give him ice cubes to lick if they are available, but *never* give an overheated dog ice water to drink. Before you set off on your journey, read your first-aid manual and become familiar with the symptoms and treatment for heatstroke and other life-threatening conditions.

If you're hiking with your dog during cold weather and you encounter a sudden drop in temperature, watch your dog for signs of hypothermia: shivering, drowsiness and lethargy. Cover him with a coat or sweater, get him quickly to shelter and warm him with blankets and warm liquids. Your first-aid manual should contain complete information on the treatment of hypothermia.

If you plan to picnic or swim at a beach where there is little or no shade for your dog, consider a "pup tent," a portable canvas shelter made of heavy-duty coated nylon. These low-roofed tents set up in minutes with fiberglass poles and have easy-to-fill sand pockets for tie-downs. The tent collapses into a small travel carrying bag. Great for kids, too!

Most camping facilities require that dogs be kept on a leash or tie-out at all times. They usually stipulate that a dog not be left tied up or left alone while its owners go off hiking or exploring. Most importantly, an unattended dog can easily be stolen. Your dog's security should be your first concern. Always take the dog along or leave someone behind to watch him.

Find out if your camping area has a lake or swimming pond. Most dogs love to romp on a beach and race through the shallow water along the shore. Retrievers and spaniels are natural water dogs and will dive into the wet stuff at every opportunity. Other breeds may

**KC Chances R Walk'n on Sunshine, owned by the author, models her own swimsuit.**

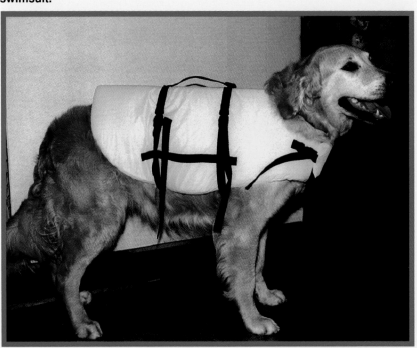

**Don't pick a camp site without a great watering hole for your active dog, especially if your dog's of the Golden variety! Lola in action, doing what every retriever is born to do!**

need a more gradual introduction to water and swimming. If your dog is a bit hesitant at first, coax him gently and be patient, but don't force him in. The sight of you playing in the water should be enough to tantalize him to take the plunge and join the fun.

**Lola, dressed to hunt, confidently holds her training bumper.**

If you plan to swim with your dog but are concerned about his stamina or swimming ability, consider using a canine life vest. A life vest will not only keep him afloat but keep him insulated against cold water. Most come in several sizes and can be purchased from pet or hunting supply catalogs or outlets.

Be prepared in case you run into bad or wet weather (heaven forbid!) on your outdoor trip. Rain means a wet dog curled up beside you and muddy pawprints across your sleeping bags. Bring extra towels just in case.

Despite a few disadvantages, dog owners insist that camping with their favorite canine is a special time for themselves and their dog. Yours will love it too!

## WHAT TO PACK FOR THE CAMPING DOG

Whether you plan to camp for a few days or several weeks, you will need the same basic equipment for your dog:

- Dog backpack (if hiking)
- Food and water bowls and canteen carriers
- Leash or flexi-lead
- Water filter kit (optional)
- Dog food, treats, and water supply
- Blanket or dog sweater
- Health records, including proof of rabies vaccination
- Tie-out chain or rope
- Flea and tick spray, other insect repellent
- Plastic baggies for stool pick-up
- First-aid manual and supplies
- Plastic spray water bottle

A canine backpack is like a saddle bag. It has large bellows pockets on each side to hold hiking and first-aid supplies, a

**A canteen designed especially for pets is easy to carry and just as easy to use. Just unhook the shoulder strap, unscrew the lid to allow your dog to refresh himself.**

**A pet-travel canteen is ideal for camping and hiking as well as a long walk around the neighborhood. Here's Sasha, getting a drink from her canteen.**

water bottle and snacks. The packs are attached to the dog by a yoke that fits comfortably over the dog's shoulders. Most are made of waterproof fabric and are available in three shapes...square or box shape, saddlebag or "U" shape, and contour design. They come in one or two pieces and are sized according to the dog's weight.

The dog's pack *must* fit properly to be safe and comfortable for your dog. A poorly fitted dog pack that sags or is poorly constructed can cause sores on the dog's back or elbows and could further injure his back and legs. If possible, take your dog with you when purchasing his pack so you won't compromise his safety and comfort on the trip.

There exists a variety of food and water containers suitable for trail use. The pet travel canteen that converts into an open water dish and comes with an

adjustable shoulder strap is ideal for taking clean water into areas where the water quality is questionable.

Your camping and hiking first-aid kit should contain all the essentials, with a few extra items specific for problems you might encounter on the trails. A snake-bite kit would be a must if you plan to visit areas known to harbor venomous snakes. Check it out with your veterinarian or someone experienced in snake habits and habitat to acquaint yourself with proper snake-bite treatment in case the worst happens.

Dog booties are a handy addition to protect your dog's pads in case of foot injury. They would be especially welcome if you're hiking over very rocky terrain. A small needle-nose pliers to remove porcupine quills or splinters is another handy tool in case your dog encounters a prickly outsider.

Tie-out stakes will help confine and control your dog when resorting at a campground or in the wilderness where it's especially important to know where your dog is at all times.

This dog is fitted with a lightweight backpack. A good rule of thumb for backpacking is that the dog should not be expected to carry more than one-sixth his body weight. This 60-pound Siberian Husky shouldn't carry more than 10 pounds in his pack for owner Wendy Willhauck.

Unless your camping facility has a water system guaranteed to be safe for people and dogs, you should bring your own bottled water. Otherwise you could boil the local water, or use a portable water-filtering system to purify the water. Today most of the free-running water in the wilderness contains highly contagious organisms and is unsafe to drink. These bacteria can cause severe diarrhea and dehydration in humans and dogs and can be life threatening to puppies.

Most water filters are compact and easy to use and can be purchased at camping- and hiking- supply centers. Boiling your drinking water will kill any living organisms, but won't filter out the sludge or other foreign elements in the water. For safe camping and backpacking, you should be informed and prepared about the water in your destination area and make necessary preparations in advance.

There are several books available about camping with canines. If you're serious about camping or backpacking with your dog, take time out to research this adventure. It will enhance your camping pleasure.

Three Golden Retrievers, Tucker, T-Bear and Tanner, accompanied this truck hauling a live trap for bear cubs, being transported to the Los Angeles zoo. The trek was 2200 miles!

Be sure to accustom your dog to a tie-out before embarking on your trip.

## THE GREAT NEWFOUNDLAND DOG TREK

*by Ozzie Foreman*

Fifty-three hundred miles, and a month on the road camping with three dogs? The prospect of this was enough to make even experienced camper dog exhibitors apprehensive! My husband, Rick and myself, along with our two Newfoundland dogs, Spirit and Redi, and our 13-year-old American Staffordshire Terrier, Kitty had decided to join the Great Newfoundland Dog Trek. The Trek would consist of a caravan of recreational vehicles (RVs), traversing Newfoundland. This pilgrimage would transport over 100 Newfoundland dogs (affectionately called Newfs) to take part in Newfoundland's Cabot 500 Celebration commemorating the 500th anniversary of John Cabot's voyage to Newfoundland and elsewhere in Canada. A replica of Cabot's ship, the Matthew, was constructed in Bristol, England and retracked his voyage, docking at Bonavista, Newfoundland on June 24, 1997.

Trekking with dogs, the adventurous Newfoundland fanciers tour the Matthew, the replica of the ship John Cabot voyaged from England to Newfoundland 500 years ago.

Lloyd Nelson of Whitby, Ontario organized the Trek when he learned that six Newfs had served as mascots on the Matthew in England. Nelson thought it would be nice to have six Newfs in Bonavista to greet the Matthew on its arrival this side of the Atlantic. Nelson sent out a call on the Internet for a few other Newfs and owners to join him camping across Canada. He was overwhelmed by the response. In early June, Mike and Vivian Fritz, of Seattle, Washington joined Rod and Joan Leach in Cranbrook, British Columbia, and began the Trek across Canada. Trekkers joined the caravan at designated campgrounds along the way, until there were over 80 RVs and 130 Newfs assembled at their final destination, Bonavista.

Rick and I joined at Oshawa, Ontario in our 10-year-old Chevrolet van pulling our 20-year-old travel trailer. I had to think in terms of packing a month's worth of everything, plus, the dogs each needed proof of rabies vaccine given within the year and health certificates signed by a licensed veterinarian. In addition to taking dog crates, exercise pens, leashes and collars, I packed a month's worth of prescription medications (human and canine), heartworm

**The versatility of the Newfoundland breed became a focal point of the anniversary proceedings. Here's Carol Ralston with Ebunyzar carting—they also demonstrated flyball!**

preventative, lots of anti-diarrheal and Pink Bismuth (for humans and canines), and a well-stocked first-aid kit. The island of Newfoundland has no fleas or ticks, but to keep the abundant and vicious mosquitoes and black flies from making our dogs or us lunch, plenty of bug repellent was a must.

Experience had taught us to pack the whole journey's worth of dog food. Dog food brands are not distributed in all areas. In a strange location, finding a feed store can be diffficult. I loaded 120 pounds of dry kibble into the trailer, along with a case of canned dog food to add flavor in case the stress caused appetite loss.

The purpose of the Trek as it crossed Canada, stopping at various locals, was to promote the Newfoundland breed, and to demonstrate its unique skills. I packed our small cart, harness, and water equipment for the carting and water rescue demonstrations. Radio, TV, and newspapers covered the event at each stop. In the spotlight, Trek dogs and owners were expected to set good canine citizenship

The Matthew arrives to Bonavista on the evening of June 24, 1997.

examples. The dogs were well behaved and always on lead, and owners were expected to clean up after their dogs even in remote places or high brush.

Most of the Newfs on the Trek traveled in their crates, and many Newfs slept there at night. Camping methods were as varied as the Trekkers. Ted Mittelstadt, of Owatanna, Minnesota drove a

minivan and pitched a tent every night, no matter how cold or how bad the weather. Margie Grant, of Simcoe, Ontario, who had never camped, drove the Trek alone, sleeping in her minivan. As Margie slept, her Newfs, Lucy and Buddy, slept crated outside. Peter and Pauline Buchan, of Collingwood, Ontario towed and pitched a fold-down camper. The majority of the Trekkers used various-sized travel trailers and motorhomes. Don and Julie Sharkey and Pat and Steve Escalante rented class C motorhomes specifically for the Trek.

The Trekkers' RVs were loaded aboard the ferry at North Sydney, Nova Scotia, with TV and newspaper coverage. Marine Atlantic Ferry routinely transports dogs in their kennel, but the company gave special dispensation to Trekkers allowing the dogs on the upper observation deck for the five-hour voyage.

In Port Au Basques, Newfoundland, the Newfs finally set foot on their homeland. Newf Trek had to cross the 700-mile-long island to Bonavista on the east coast. There are very few Newfoundland dogs on the

This custom rig transported Moose and Tasha and their owners Mike and Vivian Fritz to Newfoundland from their home in Seattle, Washington.

island; and amazingly, most Newfoundlanders have never seen a live Newfoundland dog. The Trek's first scheduled demonstration was at the Corner Brook Mall. Trekkers with sulky type dog carts gave cart rides to children for a donation to charity. Other Newfs posed with admiring spectators and enjoyed petting sessions. Dogs and owners were invited inside the mall for more celebration and the town's unveiling of their scale model of the Matthew.

Though the Matthew was slated to sail to Newfoundland, then spend the summer sailing

A local Newfoundland resident, L. Roberts, joined the proceedings with this super cart and his dog Lady.

The organizer of the Great Newfoundland Dog Trek, Lloyd Nelson and his dog Blue provided rides for excited youngsters at the celebration in Newfoundland.

the Matthew as it docked. My Newf, Spirit, was chosen as one of these six.

The Trek's final stop was the large city of St. Johns. The Trekkers demonstrated draft work on the wharf, while the Newfs and owners took sailing tours of the harbor aboard the schooner "J and B." The ship took 21 Newfs, including the ship's own mascot Newf, Sailor, sailing. On July 1, Canada Day, the Trek ended with the finale of a "Super Dog Carnival" featuring the Companion Dog Trainers Ltd., showing agility, then Carol Ralston and her Newf, Ebunyzar, demonstrating flyball, then holding a flyball workshop.

Groups of any breed fanciers can organize a similar trek. They

from harbor to harbor around the island, Bonavista would be its first landfall. The celebration would be crowned by visits from Queen Elizabeth II, Prince Philip, the Prime Minister of Ireland, the President of Italy, and other dignitaries. Our 130 Newfs formed an impressive honor guard lining both sides of the path walked by Queen Elizabeth II and the dignitaries after a park dedication the morning of June 24. Six Newfs would form the welcoming honor guard that afternoon, as the Queen greeted

Rick Roseman with his dog Redi at Paradise Farm.

do not have to take Alaskan Malamutes to Alaska, or Chesapeake Bay Retrievers to Chesapeake Bay. Scottish Terrier or West Highland White Terrier fanciers could form a trek to Nova Scotia for one of their Scottish festivals for example. All it takes is a little creativity and a lot of planning. Learn from the Great Newfoundland Dog Trek's mistakes. Hire a professional travel agent, or have someone, who lives in the area, check out campgrounds long before the event. Have this person draw up precise directions to each stop, and perhaps arrange large group discounts with the campgrounds. The Newf Trek had many bad directions, did not travel convoy fashion, and Trekkers were constantly getting lost. Trekkers had to buy "their uniform," campground sites, meal tickets, etc., piecemeal. Requiring a several hundred dollar fee initially, then presenting each Trekker with a package containing required clothing, name tags, campground confirmations, tickets, a printed schedule, and maps would have reduced frustrations. A planned picnic, barbecue, or pot-luck dinner early in the trek would have promoted a team feeling and introduced the Trekkers to each other. Organizers should also appoint someone with experience to handle the media and public relations. Dog breed treks are a new concept. Meeting the Queen of England, thanks to Spirit, will be one of the highlights of my life. The Great Newfoundland Dog Trek happens every 500 years. Newfoundland owners hope that the next Trek will be as much fun!

**Guest author Ozzie Foreman with Spirit and Redi and 11-year-old Michael Bradley.**

Redi is ready for a schooner ride at St. Johns.

Queen Elizabeth II and invited dignitaries greet the Trekkers and their dogs on the morning of the arrival of the Matthew.

# FIRST AID ON THE ROAD

A well-equipped canine first-aid kit is an essential part of your dog's travel bag. It should contain the same medical supplies that you keep available at home in case your dog has an accident or emergency.

Basic supplies include a first-aid instruction book, rectal thermometer, Panalog® or other antibiotic ointment, syrup of ipecac to induce vomiting, Kaopectate® to control diarrhea, eye wash and ointment, hydrogen peroxide and alcohol, petroleum jelly, gauze pads and non-stick bandages, adhesive tape and vet wrap (a self-adhesive gauze

bandage wrap), cotton balls and cotton swabs, tweezers, eye dropper, a syringe without the needle for giving oral treatments, and a muzzle (a leash, tie or pantyhose). Most of this material will serve double duty in case of human emergencies, so it's a most worthy travel investment.

Be sure to read your first-aid instruction book *before* you leave. You should know basic first aid and life-saving technique if you have to meet an emergency head-on. What would you do if your dog cut himself while running through the woods, choked on a chicken bone he found at a picnic

area, or developed a sudden case of heat prostration? If your dog has a serious accident and you're miles away from a veterinary clinic, your response time in that emergency situation could literally save your dog's life.

The following guidelines are just that...guidelines. Read your first-aid manual for complete instructions on emergencies.

### CHOKING

Lay the dog on his side and restrain him in that position. Wedge something between the dog's molars on one side of his mouth to keep it open. The handle of a tool such as a screwdriver would work well. Examine the roof of the mouth and back of the throat, even between the teeth to determine if any foreign body is lodged there. Pull the tongue forward and to the side to see if there's something on the back of the tongue. Pull gently and carefully to avoid being bitten. If you discover a foreign object, use your fingers or a long-nosed pliers to maneuver it out of the mouth. If you are unable to remove it, pick up the dog and hold him upside down by his rear legs and underbelly (not recommended for large dogs). Shake him sharply to attempt to dislodge the object.

If that is unsuccessful, kneel over the dog's midsection facing toward his head. Apply pressure with sudden and forceful strokes at the base of the breastbone. Use your fist on a small dog, your knee on a larger one. If the dog does not resume breathing, proceed to give artificial respiration (mouth to nose resuscitation).

Keep or place the dog on his side and pull his neck forward. Open his mouth to make sure there is no food or other matter

**Learning CPR is recommended for every dog owner. Emergencies and mishaps cannot be predicted and only scarcely avoided. It's always best to be prepared. Photograph courtesy of Judy Iby, RVT.**

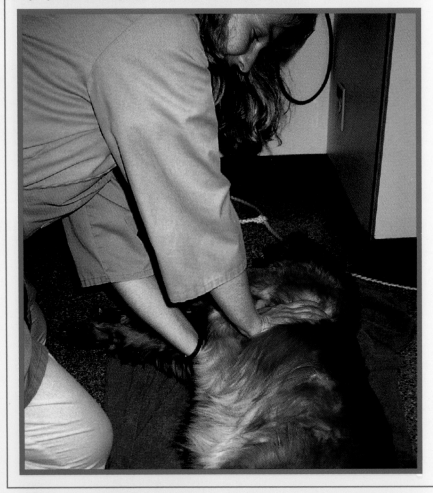

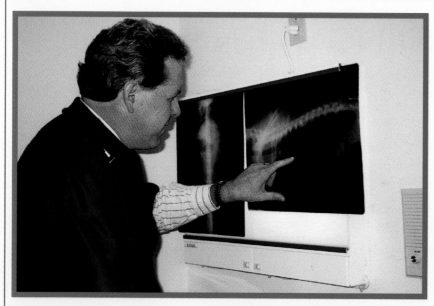

It is a good idea to x-ray the chest and abdomen of any dog that has been hit by an automobile, regardless of how "normal" the dog is acting.

obstructing the air passage. Now close the mouth and hold it while you place your mouth over the dog's nose. Slowly blow air into the nose at counted intervals until you see the chest expand.

## CPR

To administer CPR to your dog, place him on his side and kneel behind his back. If the dog is large, place one hand on top of the other over the heart at the edge of the rib cage just above the elbow, and press downward on the chest. (For very small dogs place your thumb on one side of the chest and your fingers on the other side, then compress the chest by squeezing.) Use rapid chest compressions of about 100 per minute. Stop the pressure every 30 seconds and place your hand over the heart to see if the heartbeat has returned.

## MUZZLING

If you have to muzzle your dog during an emergency to protect yourself or other rescue workers from a panic bite, you can use the dog's leash, a necktie or a pair of pantyhose. Slip the center length of muzzling material around the dog's nose and make a closed loop with a half knot on

top of the nose. Make a second loop around the muzzle so that the next half knot is under the jaw, then snug the loop and pull each end around the dog's head behind his ears. Fasten by tying a tight bow knot or bow behind his head and ears.

## AUTOMOBILE ACCIDENT

If your dog has been hit by a car, you need to transport him carefully to prevent further injury and minimize his pain. You can create a stretcher from a large towel, blanket or coat. Place the garment on the ground beside the dog. Firmly grab the scruff of his neck and pull him gently onto the garment. Lift at both ends of the stretcher to carry the dog to a safe area.

## HEATSTROKE

Heatstroke is the most common warm-weather emergency both at home and on the road. It is treacherous and life threatening and is often the result of owners' leaving their dog unattended in a car parked in the sun (often with the windows rolled down several inches). Without immediate treatment, the dog will suffer permanent brain damage and ultimately

death. The dog's body temperature must be lowered at once if the dog is to be saved. If a veterinarian is not immediately available you will have to provide that vital initial life-saving treatment.

Soak the dog with cool water from a garden hose or submerge him in a lake or stream. Completely soak the dog, especially his head and neck, for at least 30 minutes. You have to lower the temperature back to a normal 101.5 degrees. Once that is accomplished, the dog must be rushed to the nearest veterinary clinic to make sure he can maintain his normal body temperature. Most dogs who are affected by heatstroke will frequently spike temperatures back up to dangerous levels during the next 48 hours. It's imperative that you seek veterinary help at once to closely monitor the dog. Many dogs who survive those first critical hours lose the battle for life because their temperature raged out of control within that subsequent critical period. *Never* leave your dog unattended in your car during warm weather.

**Before the sun strokes! This Border Collie is standing in his lightweight crate that provides shade and "air-conditioned" comfort. The black plastic mesh provides sun protection and allows 360-degree airflow.**

# BOARDING KENNELS

Inevitably there will come a time when you must board your dog. Your vacation destination may have a pet restriction or your pet might be too old to enjoy a lengthy trip. Or you may have to board your pet briefly at your destination area while you tour museums or amusement parks.

If you board your dog for any reason, you need to locate a clean, efficient and reliable kennel with workers who are concerned and compassionate about the dogs placed in their care.

The Gaines Pet Care Center offers a publication called "Where to Buy, Board or Train a Dog," a national kennel directory that is published annually to assist the dog owner looking for a kennel where he may board his dog. You can order directly from Gaines Professional Services, P.O. Box 9001, Suite 23-1, Chicago IL 60604-9001. The American Boarding Kennel Association can also help you find a kennel in your home area or at your destination. Other pet owners are also a good resource for boarding kennels...who do they trust with their beloved dog or cat? Once you have a few names, check with the health department for

possible problems, and check with the Better Business Bureau to see if any complaints have been registered against the kennel.

Special accommodations often are available in popular tourist areas where dogs are not allowed. Yosemite National Park does not permit dogs in the hotel, lodge or park camps, but does offer kennel care at the Valley Stables in the park. Other popular tourist sites that offer pet facilities include the Circus World Museum in Baraboo, Wisconsin, Cypress Gardens, Kennedy Space Center, Sea World, Walt Disney World and Disneyland, Busch Gardens and Carlsbad Caverns.

If you are boarding your dog at home, once you locate a kennel in your area, you should make an appointment to visit the kennel to determine if it's clean, safe and properly supervised and if the facilities are adequate for your pet. Inspect the entire facility, and if the kennel staff is hesitant about opening or showing you the quarters where your pet will be housed, take your pet elsewhere. Make a list of questions so that you don't forget important issues to cover with the kennel staff.

Are the kennels and exercise areas clean? Do they smell like they are cleaned regularly? Do the dogs have access to outdoor runs and are these areas properly fenced? Are the animals exercised individually and how often? Do the dogs receive personal attention? Can you pay extra for special treatment? How often are the animals checked and by whom? Does a qualified person check the dogs at night? Is there a veterinarian on call? What does the kennel facility feed the boarded animals? Are you allowed to bring your own food and your dog's toys? (Having something that smells like home can be comforting to him while you're gone.)

What are the management's health regulations? Do they require proof of rabies and distemper vaccination or immunization against kennel cough? Kennel cough is a highly contagious upper respiratory infection, and, for your dog's safety, he should be vaccinated against kennel cough regardless of the boarding facility requirements.

Are the kennel personnel friendly and pleasant and appear genuinely to like dogs? You don't want surly people looking after your best friend.

A dog who has been well socialized and exposed to new situations throughout his lifetime should adapt well to boarding. If your pet is apprehensive, you might board him for a few overnight stays prior to your trip to acclimate him to the kennel environment. Also inform the kennel operator if your pet has any special problems or conditions, like deafness or fear of thunder. The kennel should offer a boarding agreement that details the responsibilities of the facility and the dog owner. Always read it carefully before signing.

**Sparky the Beagle enters his crate on the way to the airport. If you're unable to travel with your dog like Wendy Ballard, you will need to locate a quality, trustworthy boarding facility for your dog. Photograph courtesy of *DogGone™* newsletter.**

Don't leave home without it—be sure you bring your dog's favorite toys, including his Frisbee® from Nylabone®. Especially if you're off to a resort where there's lots of open space and time to run and play with your dog, Frisbees are essential!

# AIRLINE TRAVEL

Is air travel the best way to transport your dog? What can you expect if you ship your dog by air? Are some airlines safer than others for shipping dogs?

Despite the thousands of dogs who fly safely every year, most people still are apprehensive if their dog must travel by plane. The Humane Society of the United States emphasizes that although over 275,000 animals fly without incident every year, there are still risks involved in air transportation, and because of this they recommend that pet owners avoid air travel for their pets unless it's absolutely necessary.

If you decide to fly your dog to your vacation destination, you can minimize the risk to your dog by using common sense and planning the air travel portion of the trip to ensure maximum safety for the dog.

Each airline has its own rules about shipping dogs. You should check directly with the ones who service your destination area to determine what kind of pet-travel services they offer and which one will best serve your dog's travel needs.

**Air freight** is for dogs traveling without a person and operates from the cargo terminal rather than the passenger counter.

**Counter service** is a second animal package, also for unaccompanied animals, which accepts departing dogs at the ticket counter. At the destination point, the dogs arrive at the baggage claim area. American Airline calls this counter-to-counter service "Priority Parcel"; Delta Airline's similar service is called "Delta Dash."

**Dogs flying with ticketed passengers** fly as excess baggage. Some airlines allow very small dogs in the cabin but the dog must be crated in a unit that will fit under the passenger's seat. The generally accepted dimensions for a pet carrier in the passenger compartment are 8 inches high by 16 inches wide by 21 inches long. Some airlines also will allow a small dog in a soft-sided travel carrier to ride under the seat in the passenger cabin. The dog or puppy is expected to be quiet and well behaved, which can cause a few heart-stopping moments. A generous supply of chewies is a must!

**Find an airline that respects dog owners and welcomes them on their flights. There are no second-class passengers when it comes to dogs—particularly when there's a Dachshund in the cock pit!**

Check with the airline you select as to its exact carrier and dimension requirements. All other dogs, accompanied or alone, will travel in the cargo hold with the luggage.

Many dog experts do not recommend air travel for certain breeds of dogs. Short-nosed dogs, such as Pekingese, Chows, and Pugs would be especially at risk because they have short nasal passages that do not allow hot air a chance to cool before it reaches the lungs. Certainly pets with respiratory problems should not be flown in baggage compartments because the changes in pressure or the presence of occasional fumes in the compartment could make it hard for them to breathe. Dogs that are old, fragile, ill or pregnant could be at risk if flown. Your veterinarian should always be consulted before deciding to fly your dog.

Be sure to reserve a space for your dog when you make your own reservations, whether your dog will be traveling with you in the passenger cabin or in the cargo hold. Many airlines limit the number of pets they carry on each flight. Once their quota is filled, they will accept no more pets for that flight.

Although you don't pay for your suitcase, you will have to pay to fly your dog as excess baggage. Under the federal regulations administered by the United States Department of Agriculture, your dog is considered a piece of luggage that requires special handling, and you will be charged for that service when your dog flies with you. Find out what constitutes special handling by your particular airline and make sure your dog is handled accordingly. Your dog is your priority and you are paying for special or priority treatment.

Every airline requires that a dog must travel in an airline-approved plastic travel crate. It must be large enough for the dog to stand up, turn around and lie down. One dog per crate, with occasional exceptions when an airline might allow two small puppies to share a travel crate. Travel crates may be purchased directly from the airlines or can be purchased at pet and discount stores. Be sure to check the crates offered by the airline to make sure it meets your own personal safety standards.

**Before you arrive at the airport, be sure you have an airline-approved carrying crate.**

If you purchase your crate from an outside source, be sure it meets airline specifications for animal transport. Always check the hardware on the crate to make certain all the bolts are secured tightly and do not come loose when dropped or bumped. The American Dog Owners Association every year conducts engineering safety tests on the pet crates offered by each airline. Each year several crates fail in certain areas of safety or convenience.

In 1994, one type of crate that was tested had doors and latches that flew open or off when the crate was dropped. If your dog was in such a container and accidentally dropped by the baggage handler, he could end up bolting from the opened crate and running around loose and terrified on a busy runway.

A second crate tested by ADOA in 1994 had a dark-colored bottom tray that absorbed heat and made the kennel excessively warm for the animal inside, a dangerous hazard if there was a flight delay and the crate was left on the runway in the sun before loading. Overheating is the greatest threat to dogs in shipping, so ADOA urges air travelers to use crates with white or light-colored tops and bottoms to keep their dogs as cool as possible.

You can obtain a copy of the annual ADOA booklet on the safety of airline crates and airline shipping procedures by writing to Update: Airline Transportation, ADOA Inc., 1654 Columbia Turnpike, Castleton NY 12033. ADOA Members automatically receive the yearly updates with their quarterly newsletters.

Federal regulations require that an animal carrier must have a protruding rim around the sides to keep the ventilation openings unobstructed. They also mandate that crates have two dishes, or one divided dish, attached to the inside of the door that are accessible from the outside. While this may seem unnecessary on short flights, if there is a problem or flight delay, you'll feel better knowing your dog will be fed and watered.

Regulations also require that you attach a bag containing two meals of dog food to the outside of the crate. A cute message on the bag can't hurt. It's also a good idea to attach a leash (use clear, heavy mailing tape) to the outside of the crate. Write your name, address, telephone number and destination on top of the crate if you are traveling with your dog. Mark the carrier *"Live*

**Before sending for your new pups, make sure they are old enough to endure the stress of air travel and that they have had all their necessary inoculations. These Golden pups are arriving in Cuba!**

*Animal...This End Up!"* in bold letters on the top and on one side. Some dog owners also attach a bright-colored label with the dog's name and its destination. "Hi! My name is Astro. I'm on my way to Colorado on Flight #XYZ to visit my grandmother. Please be gentle; my mother worries about me!" Personalized labels attract attention and help airline personnel identify with the animal as a living creature and someone's best friend. Along with your dog's introduction, attach an envelope with additional copies of the health certificates, care instructions and the name and address of any person other than yourself who will be picking up the dog at his destination. Label the envelope accordingly.

Some dog owners also suggest putting night-reflective tape on all sides of the crate so it will show up amidst the luggage in the dark. If you use the tape in a decorative pattern, it will make the crate more noticeable. Make your dog's presence known! The extra steps you take will reduce the risk factors for your dog.

All states require that dogs traveling by air be accompanied by a veterinarian's health certificate signed within seven to ten days of departure. Dogs over six months old must also show proof of rabies vaccination. If there are any special health needs or exceptions, your vet should include it on the health certificate.

Before scheduling your flight, research flight plans and if possible, select a nonstop flight. Direct flights may involve a stop but not a change of aircraft. Most mistakes and accidents involving shipped animals occur during the transfer from one aircraft to another.

Avoid flying during peak travel hours, 4:00 to 7:00 p.m., when delays are more likely to occur. You want to minimize the possibility of your dog's crate's sitting on the runway or in the cargo hold for unnecessary or prolonged periods during busy arrival or departure times. Friday evenings and holiday weekends can also be more chaotic at airports, which increases the risk of confusion or delays. Midweek flights are safest and best for the traveling dog.

The legal temperature limits for flying live animals range between 45 and 85 degrees Fahrenheit. It's best to fly during the day in winter and in the early morning or late evening during hot summer months to escape the temperature extremes of those seasons. While the authorities restrict animal transport to these ambient temperatures in the holding section of the aircraft, there are no minimum or maximum requirements for the temperature on the runway. For dogs being loaded as baggage, kennels left on the runway in the sun are tragedies waiting to happen. Even 70 degrees on a humid day can warm a kennel sufficiently to trigger reactions in dogs with respiratory problems or other conditions. Breeders who ship regularly strongly discourage air transport during June, July and August. Airline cargo holds generally are safe once the plane has left the gate and the ventilation systems are turned on. But a delay at the gate after the dog has been loaded can easily prove fatal. A sealed cargo hold on a hot day, without ventilation, can heat up as quickly as a vehicle parked in your driveway.

On the day of departure, dogs traveling alone should arrive at the freight terminal at least two hours in advance of flight time. Most airlines require that a dog who is traveling with a ticketed passenger must be checked in at the ticket counter at least an hour before scheduled departure. You should allow enough time to exercise your dog thoroughly before placing him in the crate. Wait until the last possible moment to crate him and turn him over to the ticket agent. Loosen his collar so that he can slip his head out if the collar gets caught, and make sure his collar bears complete identification. And of course *never* put a choke chain or a muzzle on a dog when flying.

Check the bolts one last time before putting him in the carrier. As an extra precaution, fasten the door with a bungee cord attached from the bottom of the

**For air travel purposes, be sure that your dog's crate is big enough for him to be comfortable for the duration of the flight. Find out the largest size crate permissible on the flight and give your dog the extra elbow room. Owner, Sharon Celentano.**

door on the opening side to the window grill on that side of the carrier. USDA regulations require that you offer your dog food within four hours of check-in, but you can circumvent this rule by taping a plastic bag of dog biscuits to the top of the crate. The HSUS recommends that you don't feed your dog for at least four hours prior to flying, and offer only a small amount of water before he enters the carrier.

There exists a variety of preferences about what to place in the airline crate for bedding, but the most common choices are bath towels or shredded newspaper. A full roll of paper towels folded in layers also works well as padding and will absorb any accidents the dog might have.

After you have released the dog to the ticket agent, stay there until the skycap comes to take the dog. (Dogs *do not* go down the conveyor belt, and if the ticket agent tries to do so, ask to see a supervisor.) If permitted, accompany the skycap and your dog down to the baggage area. Tip generously...and hope the skycap is extra nice to your dog.

When you arrive at the boarding gate, tell the gate attendant that you're flying with your dog. (Wait until the line has cleared. You don't want to antagonize anyone who can help you keep track of your dog.) Ask the agent to check the live-animal manifest to make sure your dog is listed and also to confirm that with the ground crew. (The manifest is part of the captain's final weight papers.) Stay in the waiting area and watch the baggage being loaded. Your dog's decorated crate should make it easier to spot on the luggage carriers. If you see your dog, tell the gate agent and thank him for the extra attention. If you don't see your dog and they call for final boarding, ask the attendant to please check again with the ground crew and be sure they have your dog. Explain if the dog isn't on the plane, you have no reason to go. If the gate attendant demands that you board anyway, ask to have a message sent to you onboard that the dog has been safely loaded. Always smile a lot and thank the airline personnel profusely.

If your flight originated at this airport, your dog is a "local board dog"; if you arrived on another flight, it is the "dog off flight number —." Don't be embarrassed or feel awkward about these inquiries. Your best friend is flying, and you've paid extra for his special handling. Most airline personnel, especially those who own dogs and pets, will realize your concern is natural and will try to help you in every way they can.

However, a certain number of counter and gate agents, as well as some flight attendants, may not be knowledgeable about animal transportation and may not understand or empathize with your concern. Simply pursue the chain of command until you feel comfortable about your dog's whereabouts and condition. You won't hurt any feelings, and your dog is worth it!

Concerned Golden Retriever owner Claire Caro from Ohio takes her dog's flight security program one step further. When Claire boards the plane she presents the flight attendant with a note to give to the captain. Her note explains she is flying with her Golden and she may not have been able to see the dog loaded onto the plane. She asks that he check with the ground crew and that if the take-off is delayed, to make sure adequate ventilation is maintained in the cargo hold. "Please sign and return this note to me. Thank you for the extra attention." she concludes, and signs the note, "Claire Caro, the Nervous Mother, Seat XYZ."

Claire asks the attendant to deliver the note as soon as possible. She has friends who are commercial pilots and they have assured her they want to know when they have live animals. A manifest could be wrong, and they don't ever want to lose an animal.

On several occasions after presenting her note Claire has observed the captain or first officer leave the plane and check on her dog's kennel. On one occasion an officer helped load the crate! The overall response to her concerns has been very positive, with flight attendants telling her about their own dogs, asking for training advice, etc.

Your final task upon arrival and while still on the plane is to watch to see your dog unloaded. When you deplane, thank everyone for getting your dog there safely. Your kind words will encourage them to be nice to the

Dogs have experienced air travel for nearly as long as humans—we have dogs in airplanes, helicopters and even space ships!

next dog that comes along. Then pick your dog up promptly at the baggage pickup or designated area. If your dog is flying alone, the person responsible for pick up should be in the baggage-claim area before the flight arrives and should report to the baggage-claim agent to explain that a dog is on its way. Excess baggage and small-package-service dogs come in before or after the luggage. Ask the baggage-claim agent to bring your dog in before the baggage. You might also point out that you paid for the dog but not your suitcase. If you don't see your dog within a reasonable period of time or it arrives with the rest of the baggage, request a refund since you didn't get the special service for which you paid.

If you have problems that you feel should be reported to or handled by the regulatory agency, you can contact the United States Department of Agriculture, Animal Plant Health Inspection Service (USDA, APHIS), Federal Building, Hyattsville, MD 20782.

# ONE IF BY LAND, TWO IF BY SEA

Looking for more "revolutionary" modes of travel—not automobile or airplane!? Here's some basic information about traveling with your dog by ship, bus, rail, etc.

### TRAVEL BY SHIP

Only a few shipping lines accept pets for tourist travel. With the exception of guide dogs and assistance dogs, cruise lines normally only accept animals for trans-Atlantic crossings, and these frequently require that animals be confined in designated kennels. If you must travel with your dog by ship, contact the shipping line in advance to find out their particular policies and which ships have kennel facilities. When planning a ship voyage, follow the general guidelines suggested for other modes of travel to ensure the welfare of your pet during the trip.

### TRAVEL BY RAIL

Amtrak Rail Lines do not permit animals to board their trains. A few smaller railroad companies may allow animals on board and you would need to investigate them individually. It will be the owner's responsibility to feed and exercise the animal at station stops. Pets should be prepared for travel in the same fashion as recommended for other modes of travel.

### TRAVEL BY BUS

Most bus lines do not permit animals on board. However some lines allow animals to be transported in travel crates. Check with individual bus lines for specifics.

### Assistance Dogs

Assistance dogs, such as Seeing Eye dogs or hearing dogs, that accompany their disabled owners are allowed on all trains, busses and passenger ships.

**Cruising on the open sea, this Basset Hound loves motoring about with his owner Jackie Conway.**

True to his fisherman-dog origins, the Portuguese Water Dog is most at home on the water, whether sailing, fishing or retrieving.

# INTERSTATE AND INTERNATIONAL TRAVEL HEALTH DOCUMENTATION

### WITHIN THE UNITED STATES

If you will be traveling across state lines with your dog, you should carry a current valid health certificate and a certificate of rabies inoculation. All states except the District of Columbia require health certificates and rabies inoculations within a six-month to three-year time frame

commerce or the American Society for the Prevention of Cruelty to Animals, 441 E. 92nd St., New York NY 10128.

Travel throughout the United States is unrestricted with proper documentation. Hawaii is the exception, with a 120-day mandatory quarantine for all dogs and cats.

**Crossing state lines, be sure you and your dog are prepared. No matter how appealing your dog appears, without proper documentation a dog could be refused admittance by the authorities.**

depending on the states you travel through. A few states require that the health certificate specify the type, date, manufacturer and serial number of the rabies vaccine. Although you may never have to produce your pet's health certificate at the state line, all states have the authority to refuse admittance to any animal who shows any sign of infectious, communicable or contagious disease, including parasitic and respiratory infections. Most states have various other requirements. Information on individual state travel restrictions can be obtained from their travel bureaus, a local chamber of

### TRAVEL IN CANADA

You are permitted to travel with your dog across the border into Canada as long as he has a rabies certificate issued within 12 months of your travel date. You'll also need a definitive description of your animal on or with that certificate.

### TRAVEL IN MEXICO

Travel into Mexico requires a health certificate prepared by your veterinarian within two weeks of your travel date. The certificate must include a description of your pet, the lot number of the rabies vaccine used, proof of distemper vaccine, and a veterinarian's statement verifying the animal

is free from infectious or contagious disease. This certificate must be stamped by any local office of the United States Department of Agriculture and must be certified in advance by the Mexican consulate. There is a nominal fee for this service.

### INTERNATIONAL TRAVEL

International travel restrictions vary widely. All countries require a veterinary certificate for rabies inoculation, and many for other immunizations as well. A few countries, Portugal for one, require that the vaccination certificate include the date and type of vaccination, the manufacturer, and serial number of the vaccine. Certificates must be issued from 24 hours before departure (Bahamas) to up to six months, even as long as one year in a few countries. Canada accepts documents up to three years old. Some governments, such as Germany, require an additional health certificate in their native language. Many countries require a separate veterinary certificate stating that no rabies outbreak has occurred in the area of departure during the preceding 60 days. You may also be required to carry a certificate of identification, such as your AKC registration papers.

Some regulations may also state that the rabies certificate be stamped by a United States Department of Agriculture veterinarian in the state where the dog was vaccinated. Denmark and Burundi require that the health certificate also state the animal is free of ticks. Denmark inspects the transport container and requires a veterinary inspection at the point of entry.

Most foreign countries require an International Health Certificate in addition to the current U.S. health and rabies certificate. Your dog's health passport will be written in three languages: English, French and German.

A few countries prohibit the import of any pets, even those who accompany tourists. France has a three-animal limit on dogs and cats. Some countries permit entry only if the dog has been quarantined elsewhere for six months before arriving.

Restrictions also can vary according to the country of departure. Many countries require that a tourist traveling with a dog must obtain an import certificate from his consulate, this done at the dog owner's expense. The United Kingdom and Ireland have a six-month quarantine period for dogs. In Ireland all dogs receive two rabies shots during their stay in quarantine. Egypt reserves the right to impose a 15-day quarantine at the owner's expense if the Egyptian examining veterinarian suspects

**This Rottweiler has the front seat view he deserves...**

**Given the many abilities and talents of dogs, they are frequently used by the authorities for law enforcement, drug and arson detection, and protection work. It's become a very common sight to see police dogs on the road in every city and state.**

the dog is diseased or ill. In most countries with quarantine restrictions, you must make reservations for your dog well in advance of your arrival. Guide dogs and service dogs are sometimes exempt from the quarantine restriction.

Other countries with six-month quarantine restrictions are Australia, New Zealand, Norway, and Indonesia.

To learn the specific requirements at your particular destination, you can check with the air carrier who services that country or check with the local consulate office. If the reservation clerk is not familiar with the shipping rules, insist on speaking to the freight supervisor, since in

most cases pets are shipped as excess baggage.

Regulations change frequently in many countries, so you would be wise to obtain up-to-date information before traveling outside the United States. You and your dog are subject to the law of the land you visit. You should know and understand the legal restrictions to avoid unpleasant experiences that could affect your dog's health and welfare. For more information about overseas travel, you can order a copy of the ASPCA booklet "Traveling with Your Pet" from the ASPCA Education Department, 424 E. 92nd St., New York, NY 10128. There is a nominal fee.

# INTERNATIONAL TRAVEL ADVICE

Although international travel requires a great deal of preparation and expense, it can be well worth the effort to share great sightseeing experiences with your best friend! Photograph courtesy of *DogGone™* newsletter.

When traveling abroad, always inquire about special crating requirements in case they differ from the rules that govern domestic travel. Always use the same safety precautions you employ when flying your dog within the United States.

Experienced overseas travelers suggest you pack your dog's water bottle and dish in your own carry-on bag. A small supply of water from home will be especially important during those first few hours in a foreign land. You can also pack your own supply of dog food, although most supermarkets abroad have a pet-food section.

They also recommend that you ask the freight personnel if there will be dry ice shipped on the day you plan to travel with your pet. Dry ice fumes can be deadly, and it's wise to avoid exposure on a flight of such long duration.

After your dog is checked in at the airline ticket counter, don't place him in his travel crate until the porters from the freight terminal arrive to pick him up. Be sure to ask the porters' names and introduce yourself and your dog. Tell the porters how important your dog is, to you personally and to the dog world. It's also a good idea to tip the porters...it will make an impression and provide an incentive for them to give your dog a bit of extra care and attention, an insurance policy of sorts.

Remain with your dog as long as possible, walking with the porters and your crated dog as long as you can. Then stay at the window where you can watch your dog loaded onto the plane. When you board the plane, tell the stewardess or purser that they have your pet on board and request that the captain be informed. Even if that can't be arranged, you will make an important point with the airline personnel.

Experienced travelers further suggest that shortly after boarding, you ask the steward to please check on your pet. They have no way of doing that, but it will serve to reinforce the issue of your dog's well being. Employ the "squeaky wheel" philosophy. The more people who know about your dog, the better his chances of safe travel.

As soon as you arrive at your destination, find out where the animals are unloaded. Large dogs are usually dispensed with the oversize baggage. If your dog is large or heavy, you may have to engage a porter to help you lift your dog's crate off the baggage carousel.

Release your dog immediately from his crate and walk him with you through the customs gate. Then race to the nearest strip of grass! After a long flight he'll appreciate a chance to relieve himself and slurp a drink of water from your travel pack. Most hotels in Europe will accept pets, although they may increase the room rate for larger dogs. Russia is the exception, as they seldom allow dogs in their hotels. Most European restaurants and many department stores also allow dogs to accompany their owners. The dogs, of course, are expected to be quiet and well behaved.

*Bon voyage!* You are guaranteed a great time if you embark on your chosen journey properly informed and prepared. Owner, Catherine Thompson.

# SUGGESTED READING

### TS-257
### Choosing a Dog for Life
**By Andrew De Prisco & Isabelle Francais**
384 pages, over 700 color photographs.

### TS-214
### Owner's Guide to Dog Health
**By Lowell Ackerman, DVM**
432 pages, over 300 color photographs

### TS-258
### Training Your Dog for Sports and Other Activities
**By Charlotte Schwartz**
160 pages, over 100 color photographs

### TS-197
### The World of the Golden Retriever
**By Nona Kilgore Bauer**
480 pages, over 700 color photographs

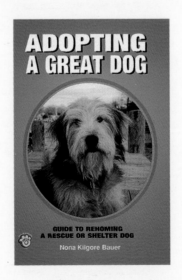

### TS-293
### Adopting a Great Dog: Guide to Rehoming a Rescue or Shelter Dog
**By Nona Kilgore Bauer**
128 pages, over 100 color photographs

### TS-252
### Dog Behavior and Training: Veterinary Advice for Owners
**Compiled by Dr. Lowell Ackerman**
288 pages, over 200 color photographs